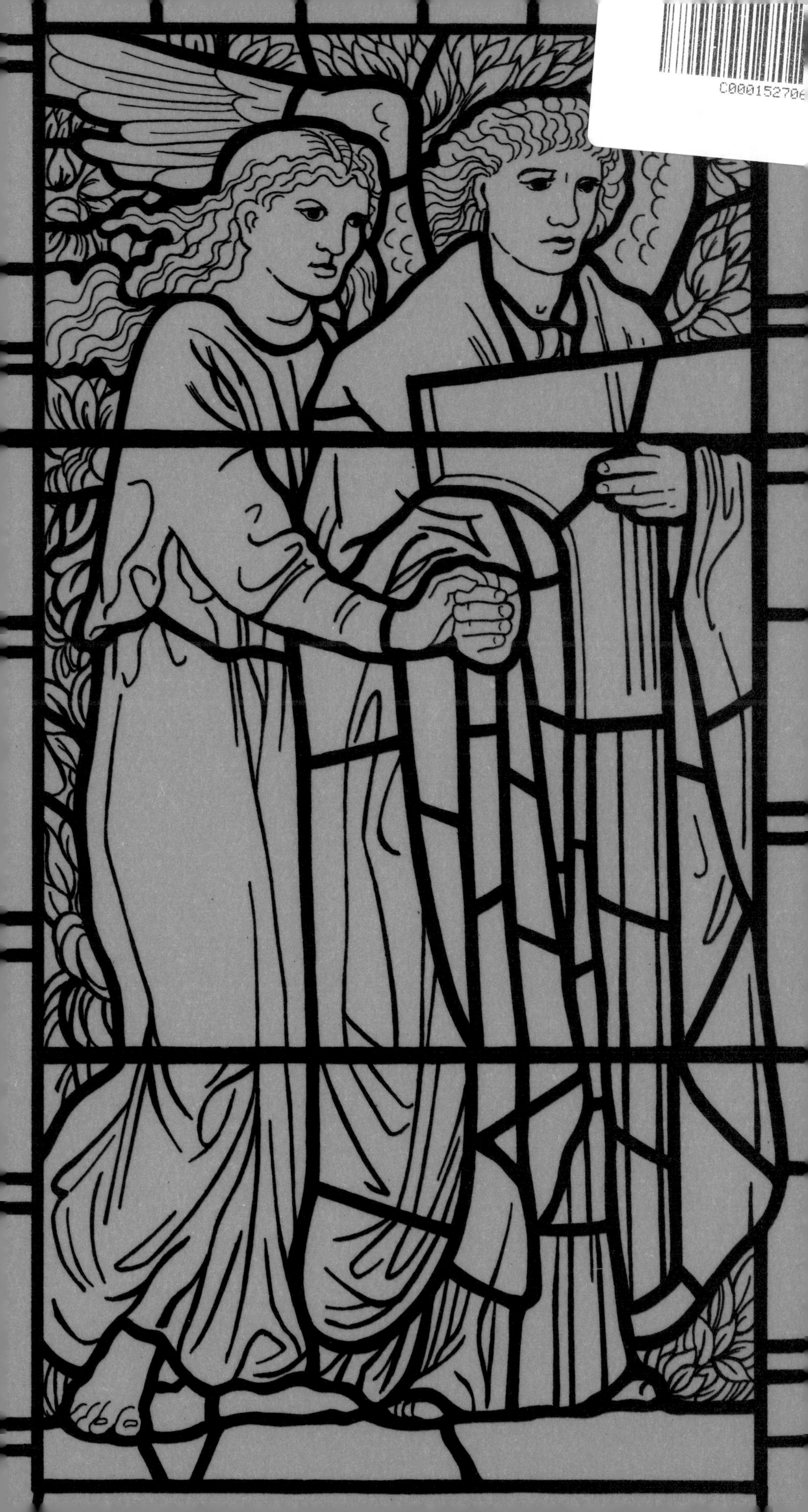

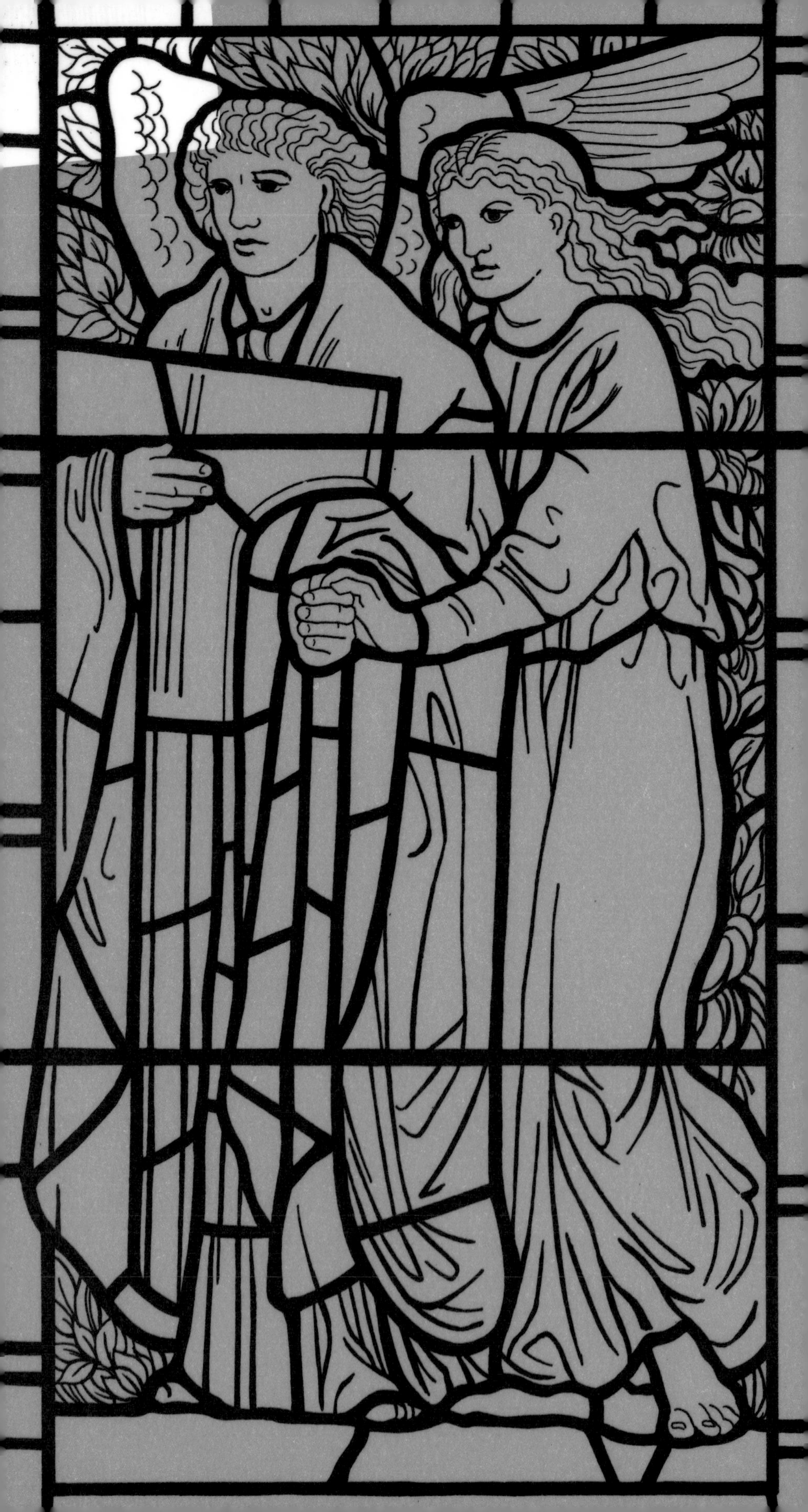

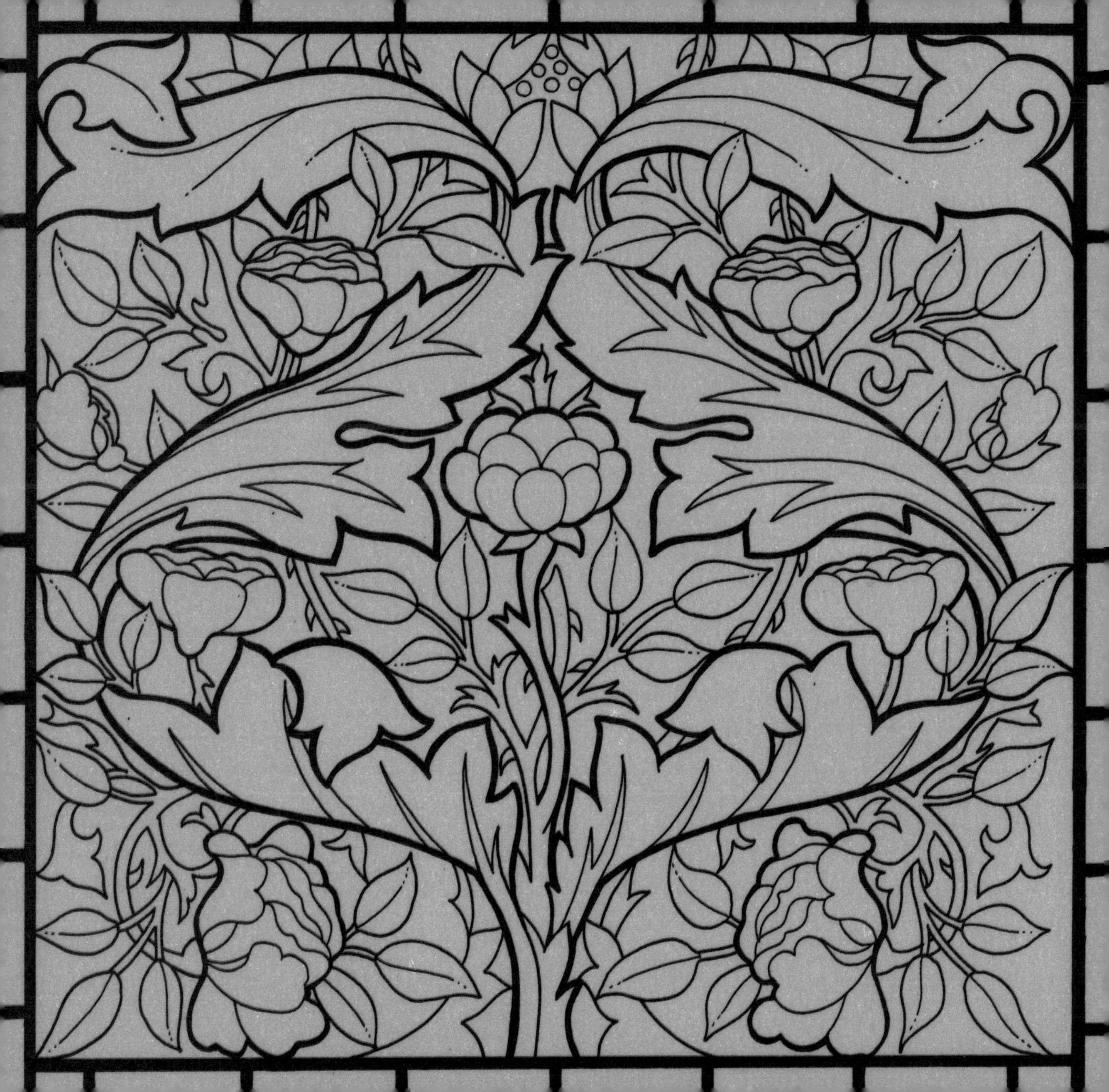

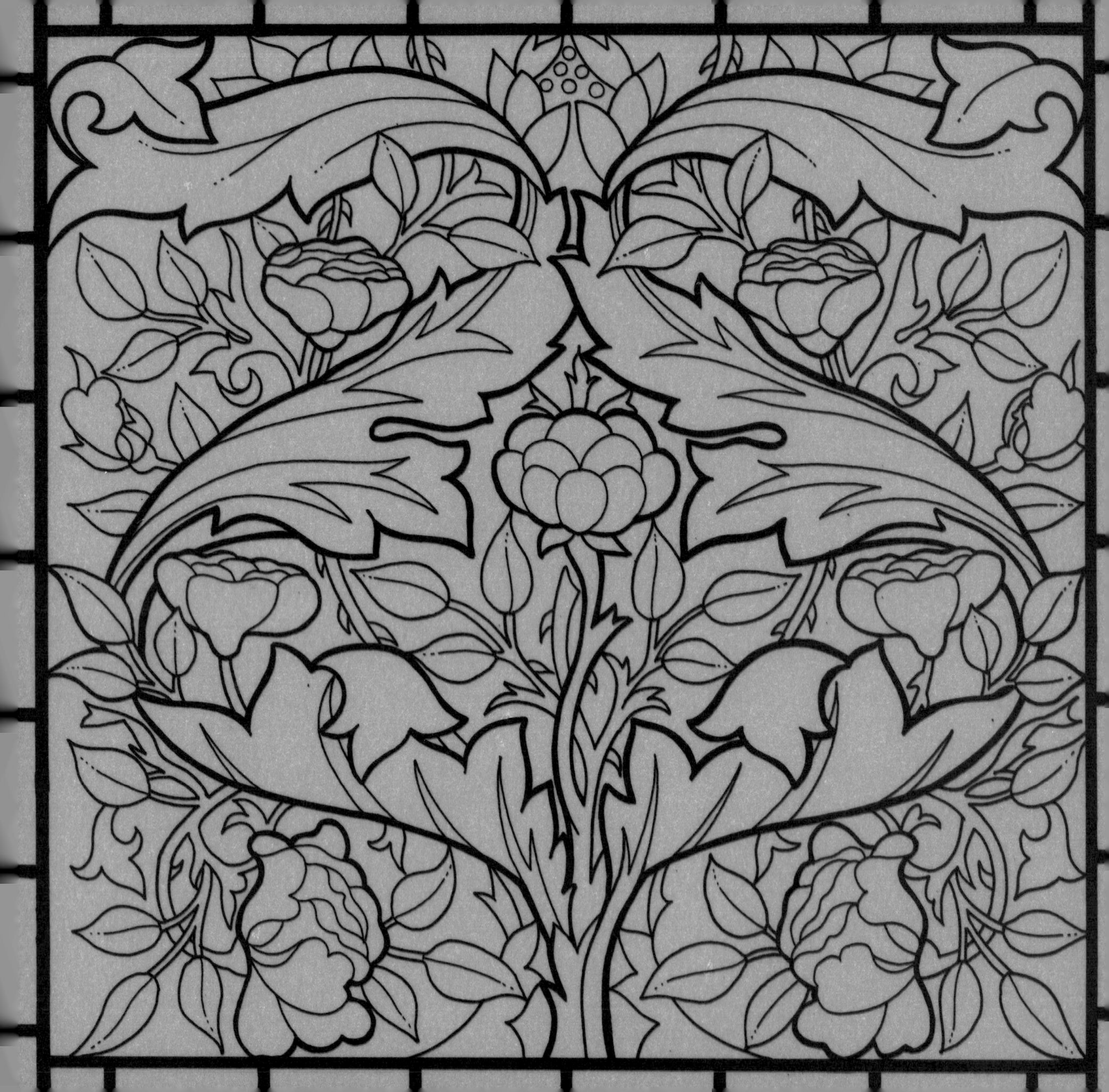

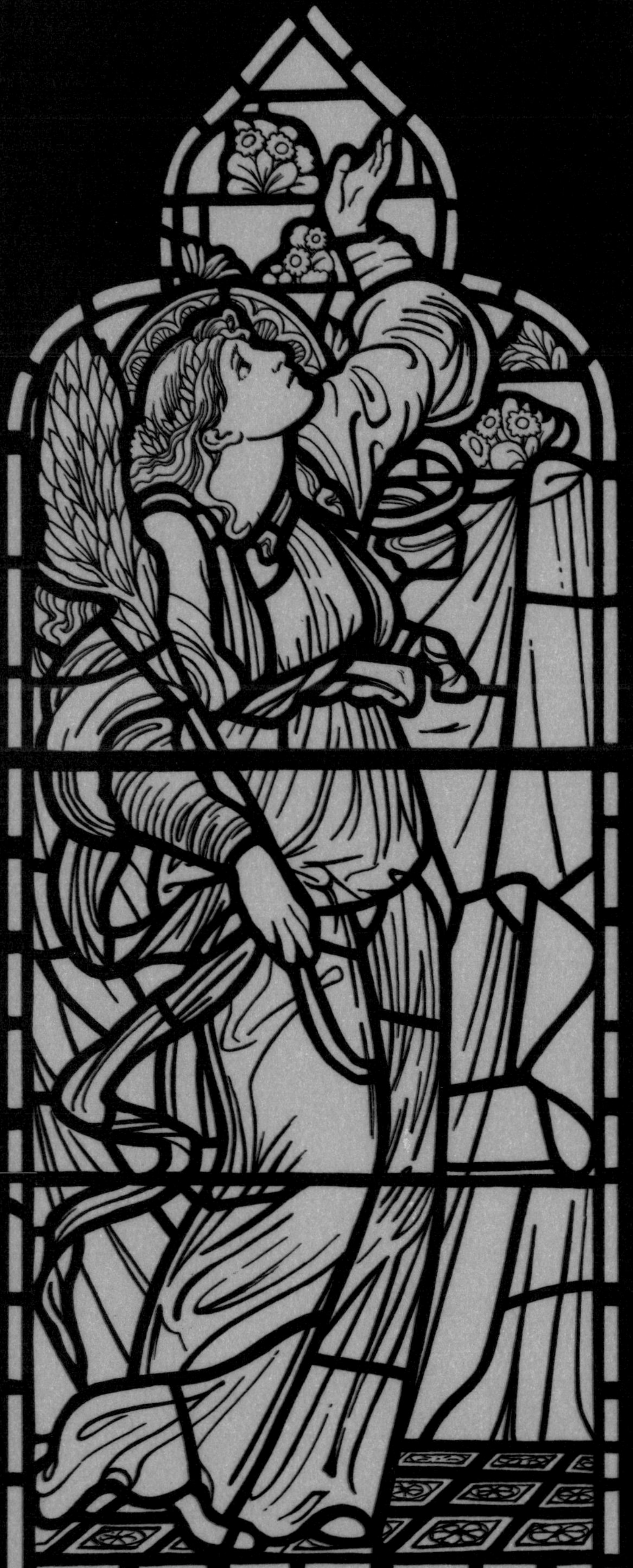

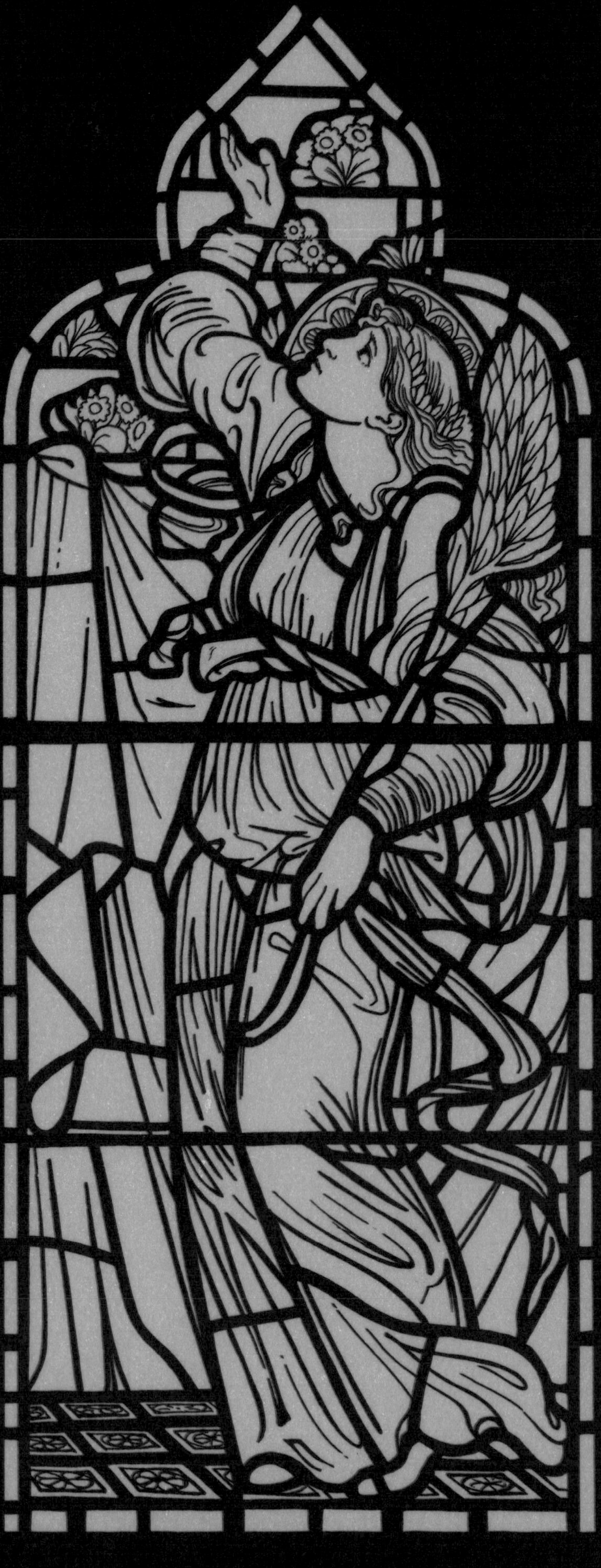

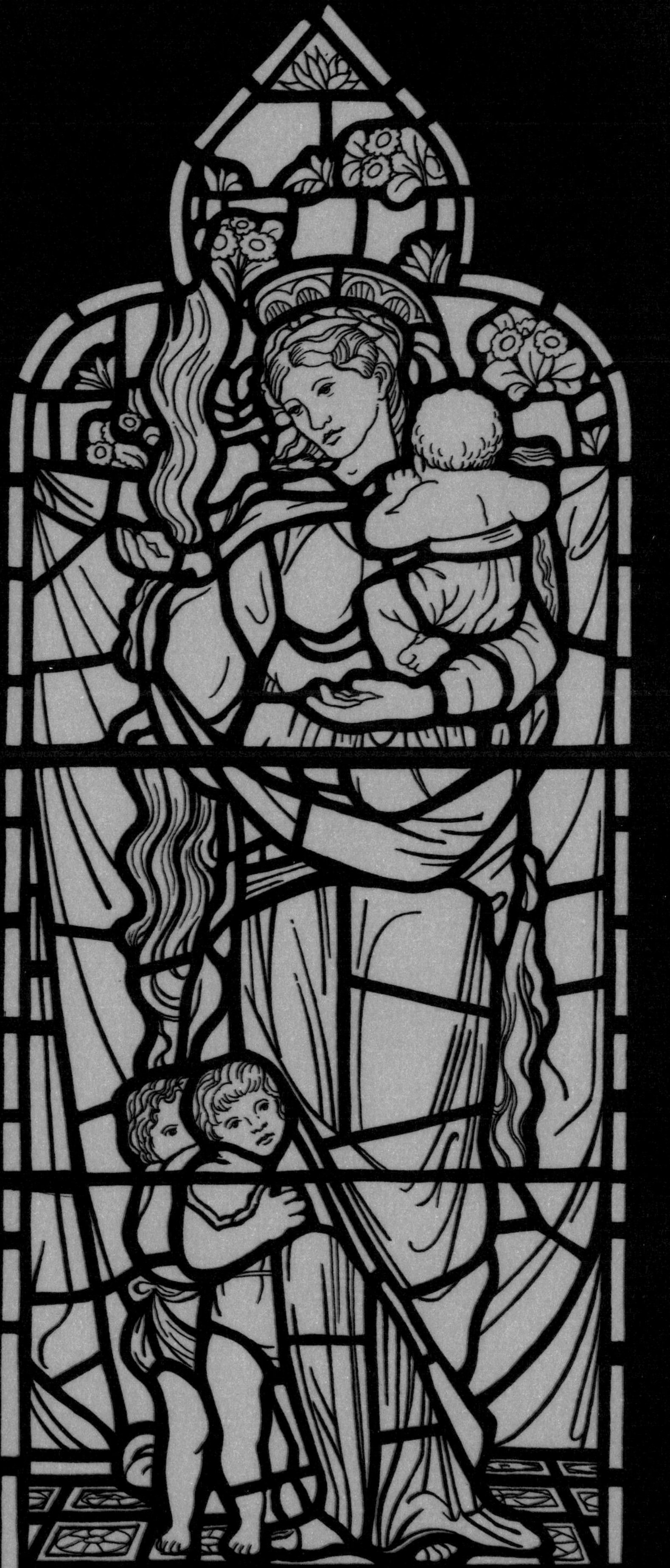

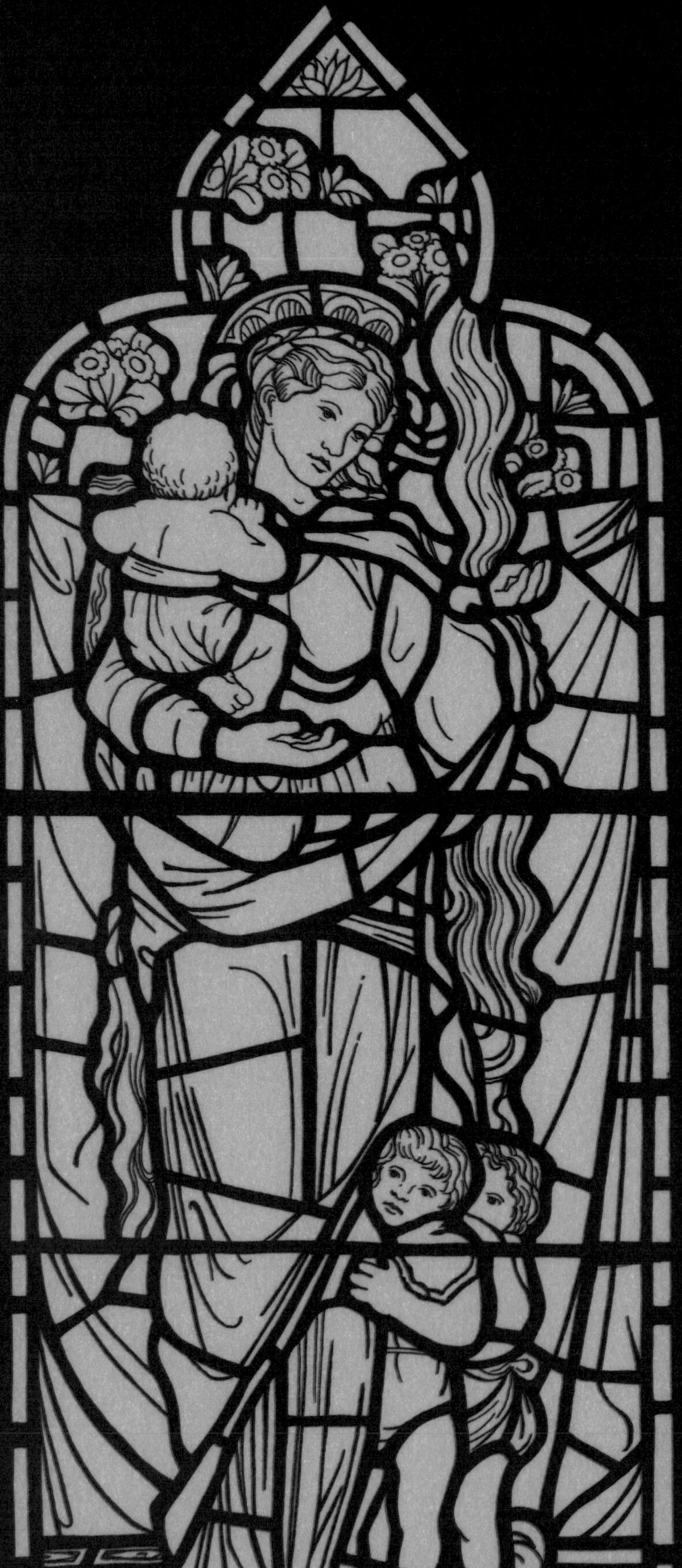

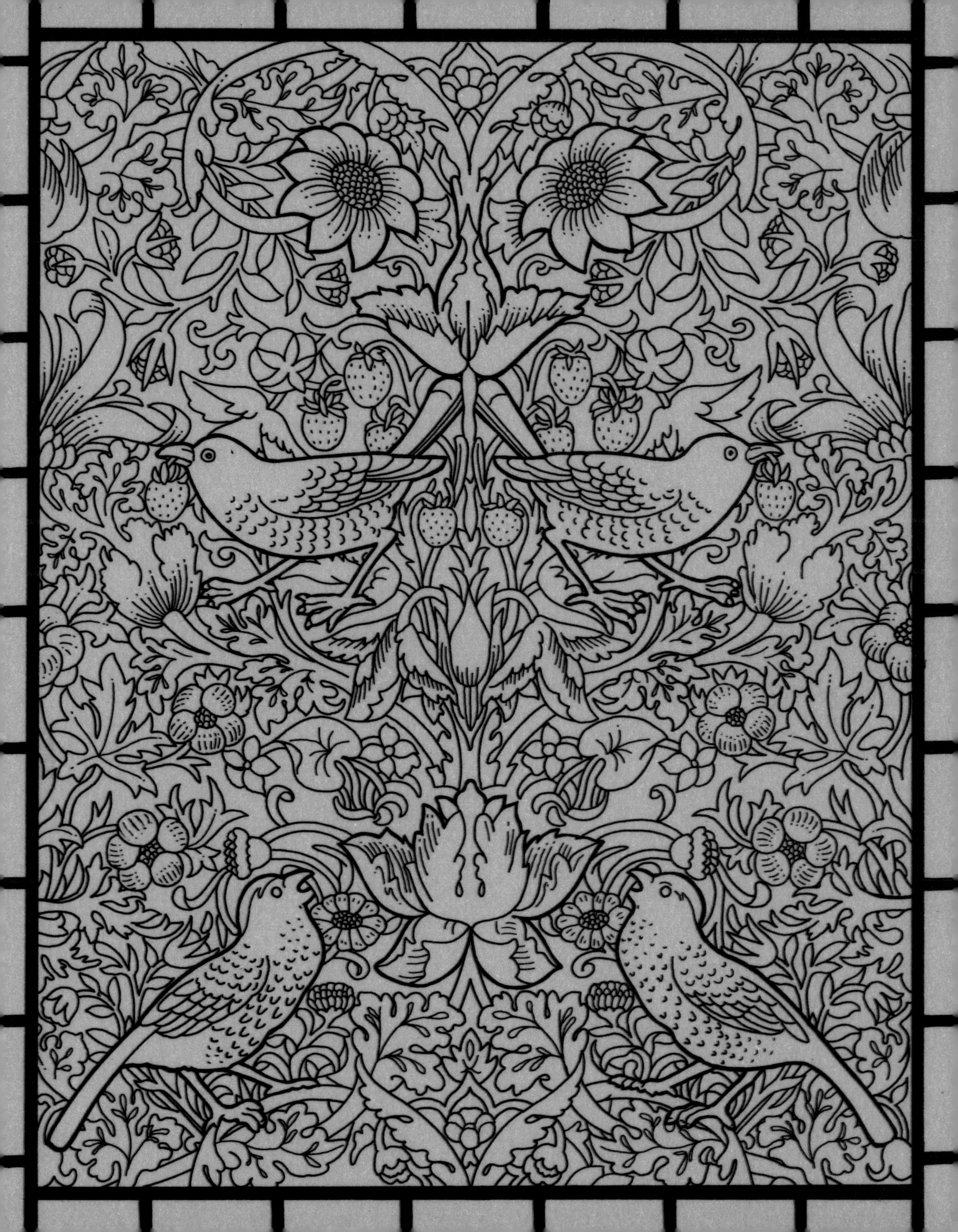

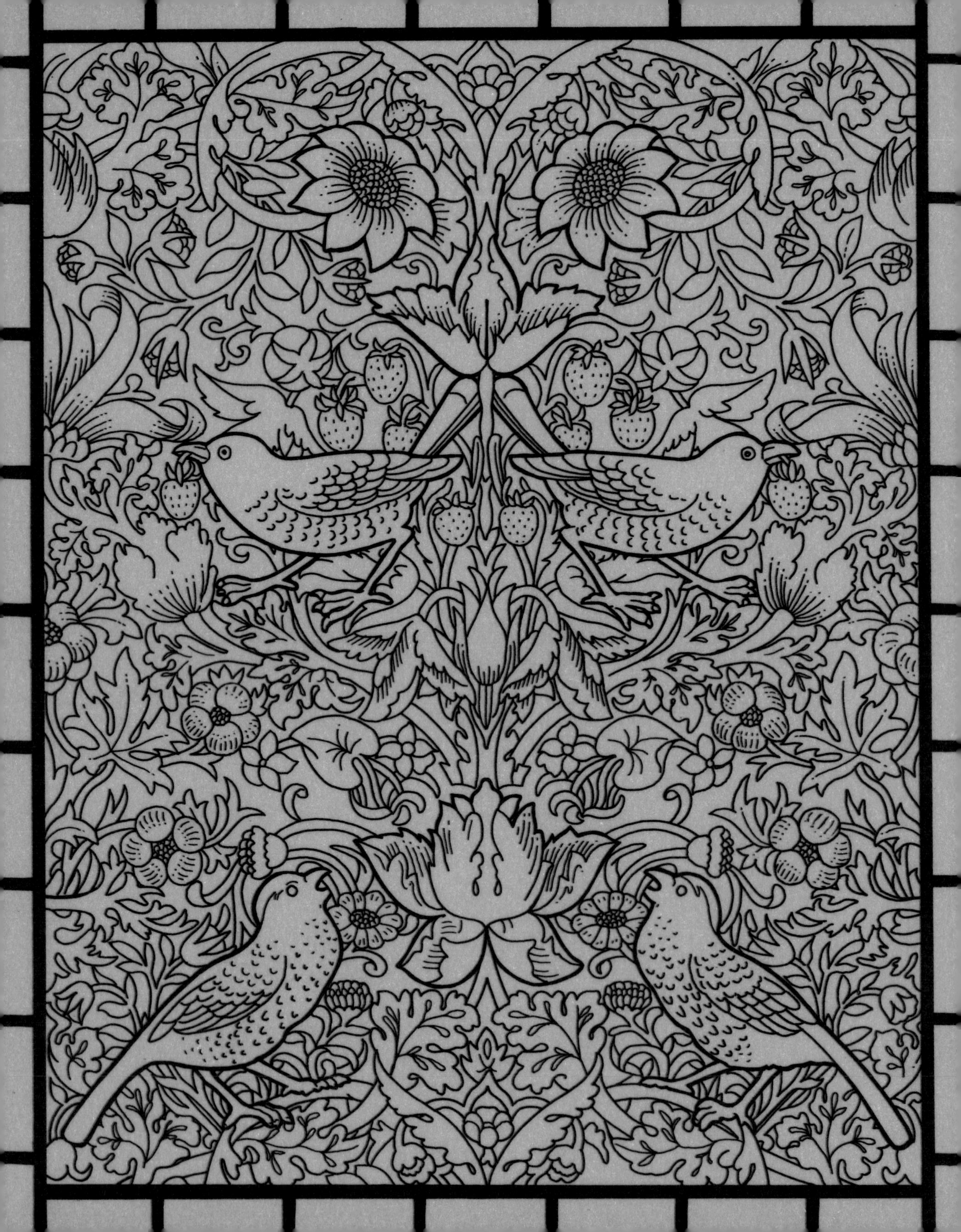

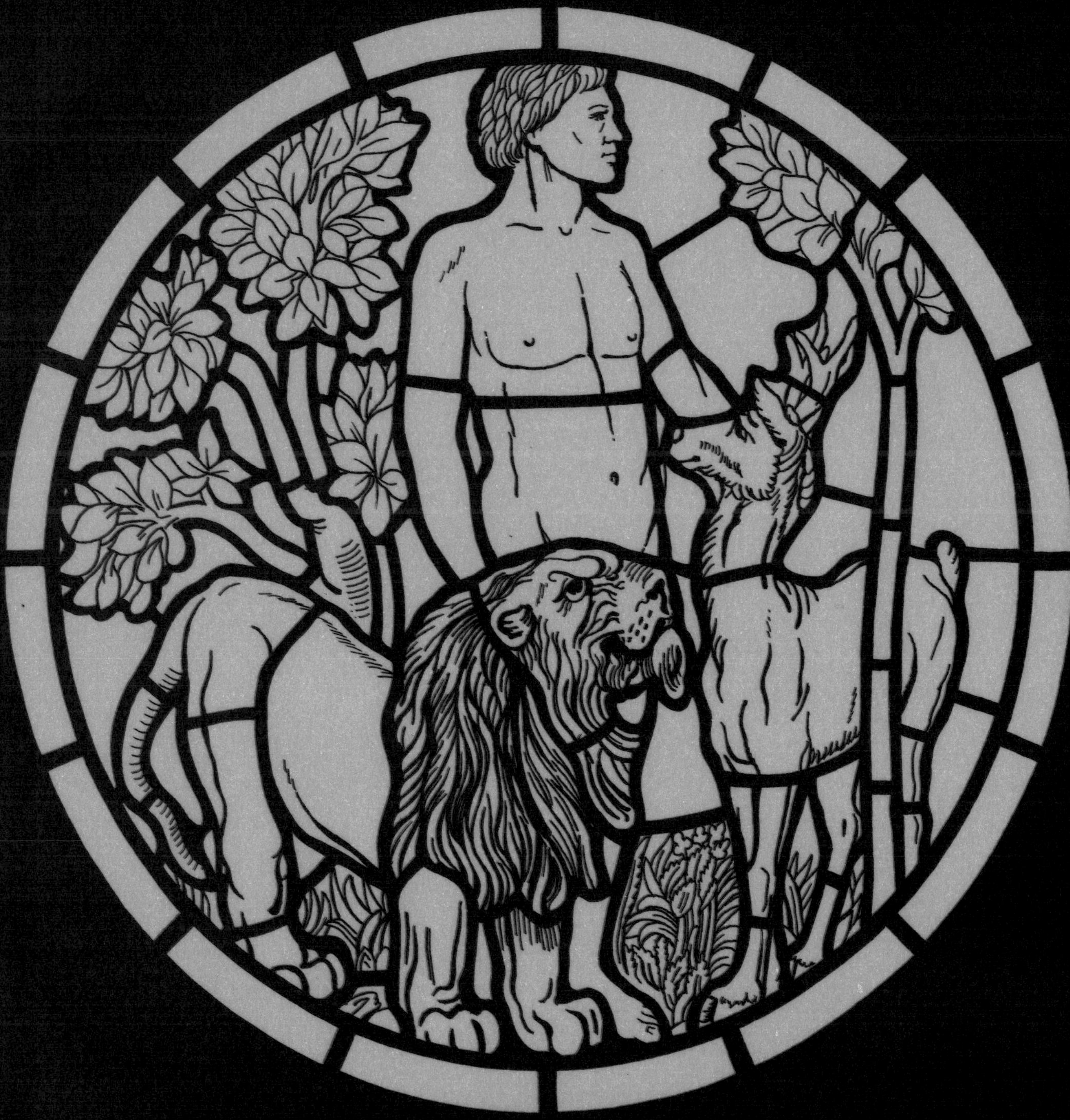

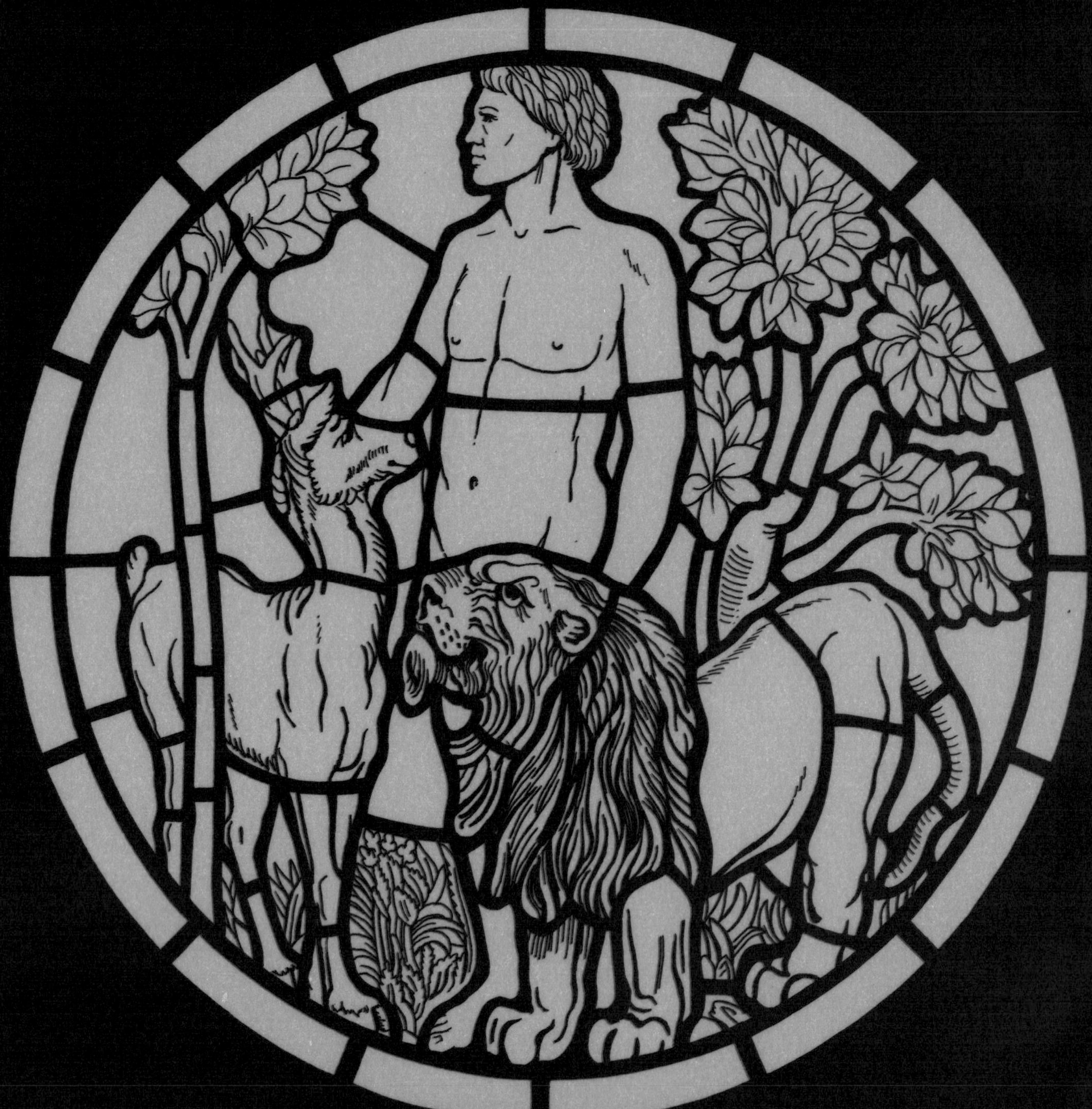

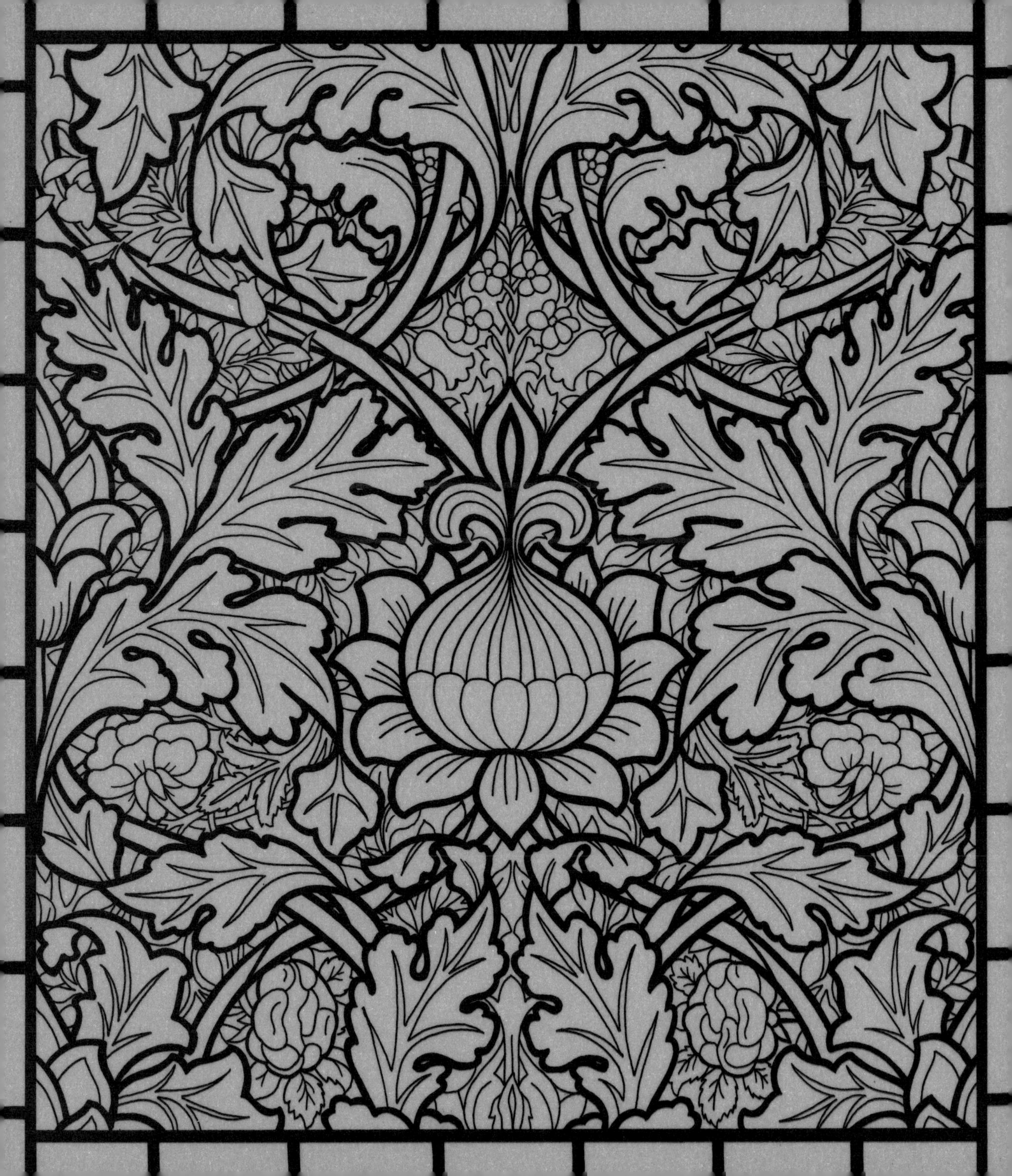

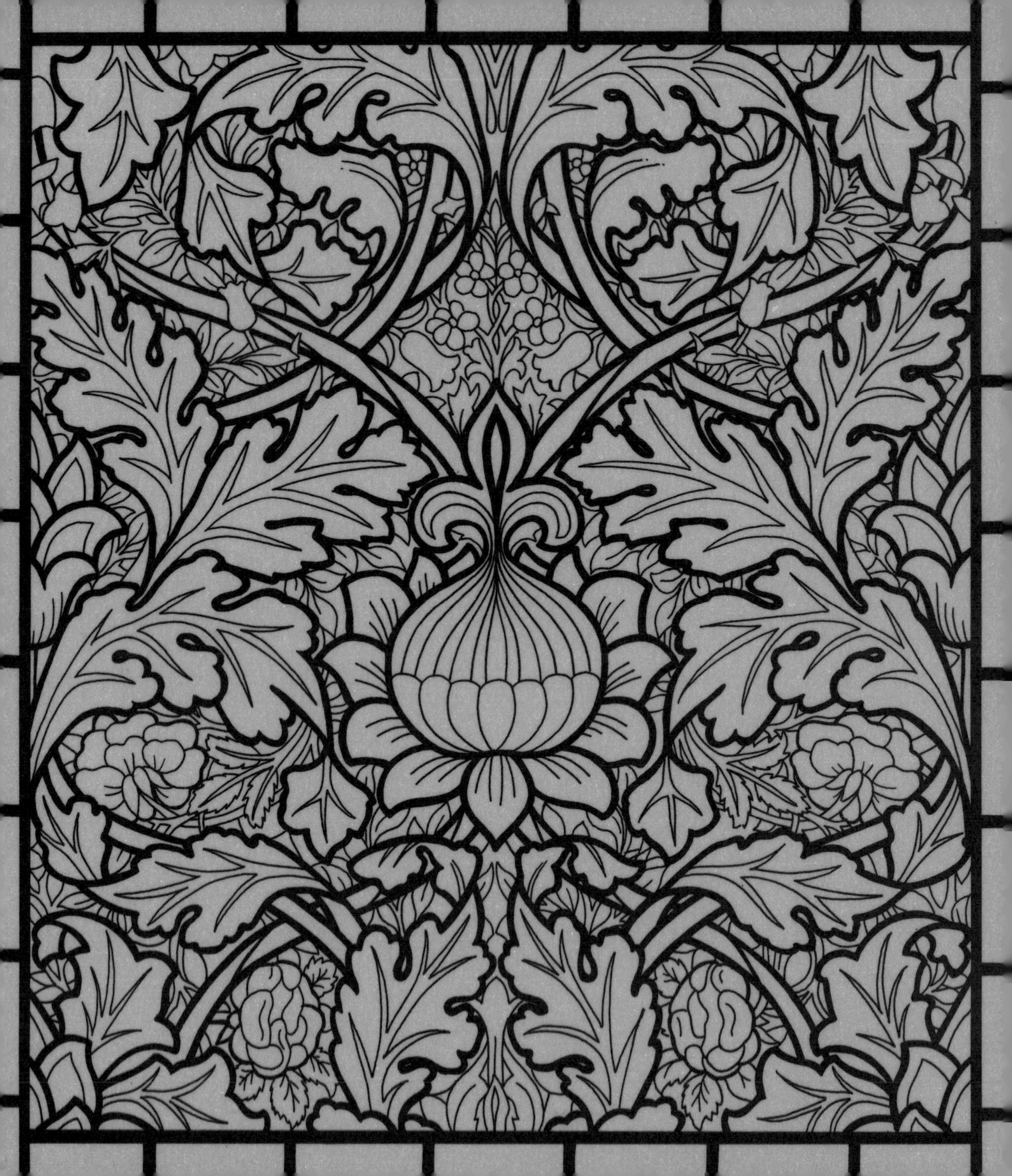

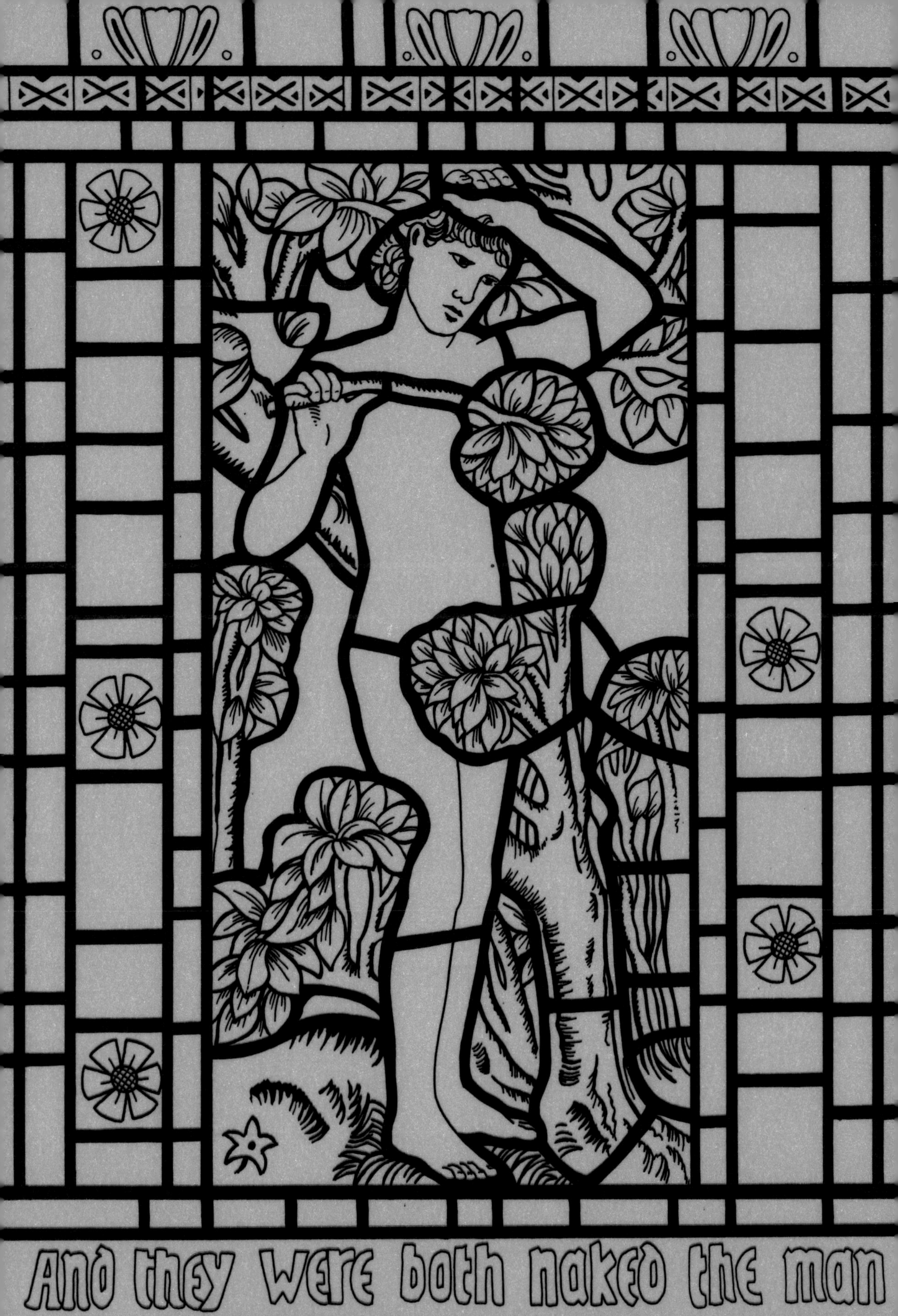

And they were both naked the man

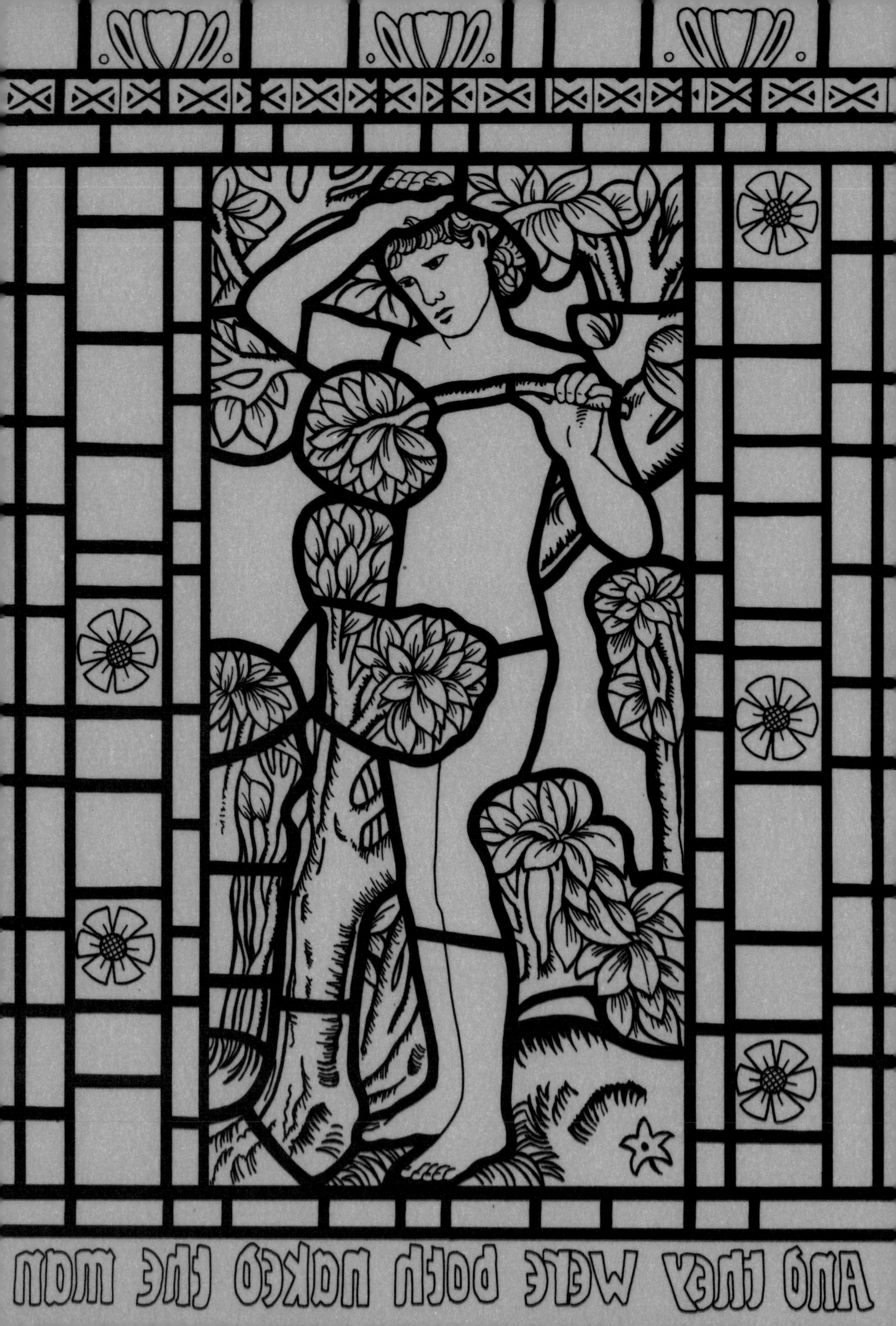
And they were both naked the man

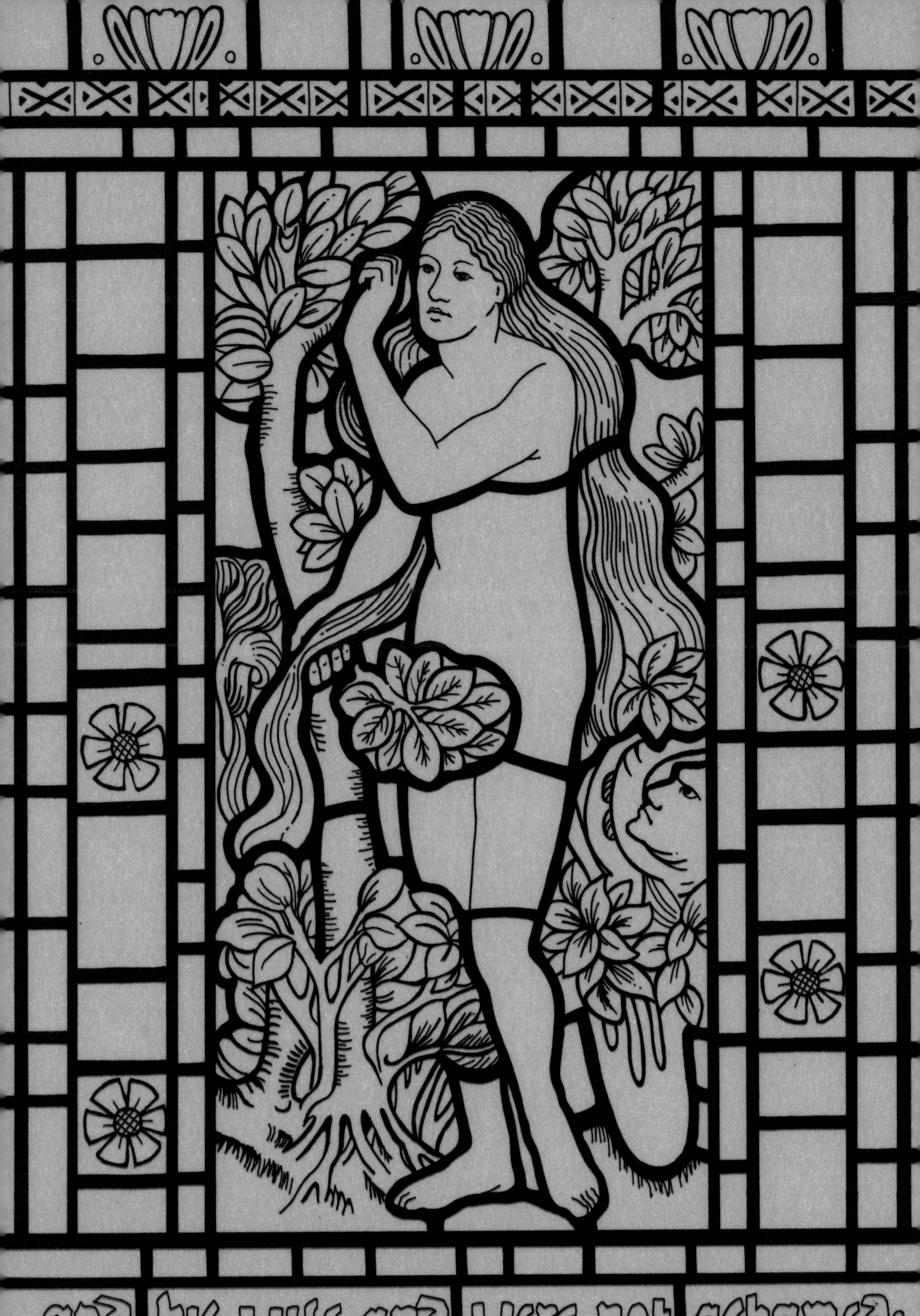

and his wife and were not ashamed:

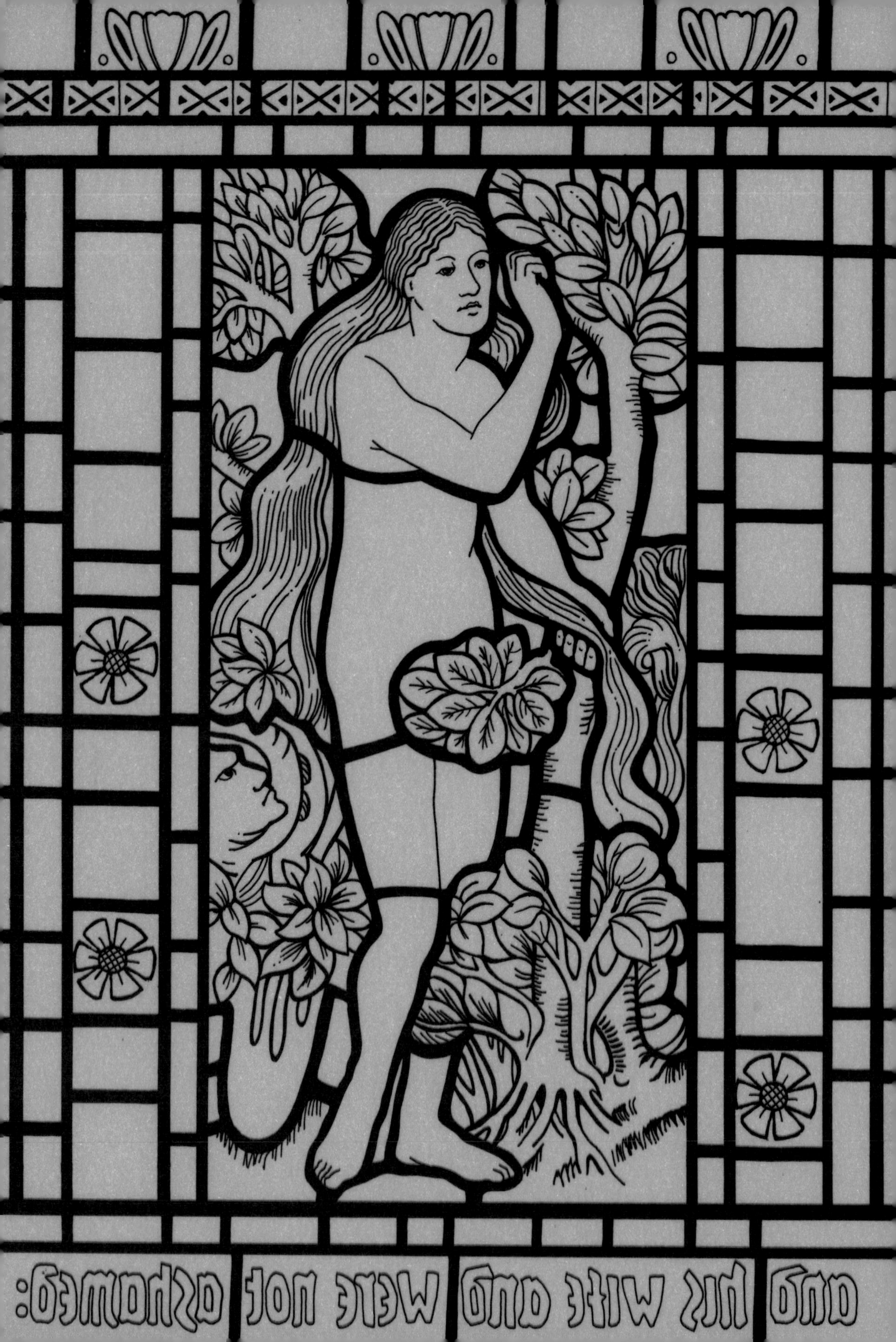
and his wife and were not ashamed:

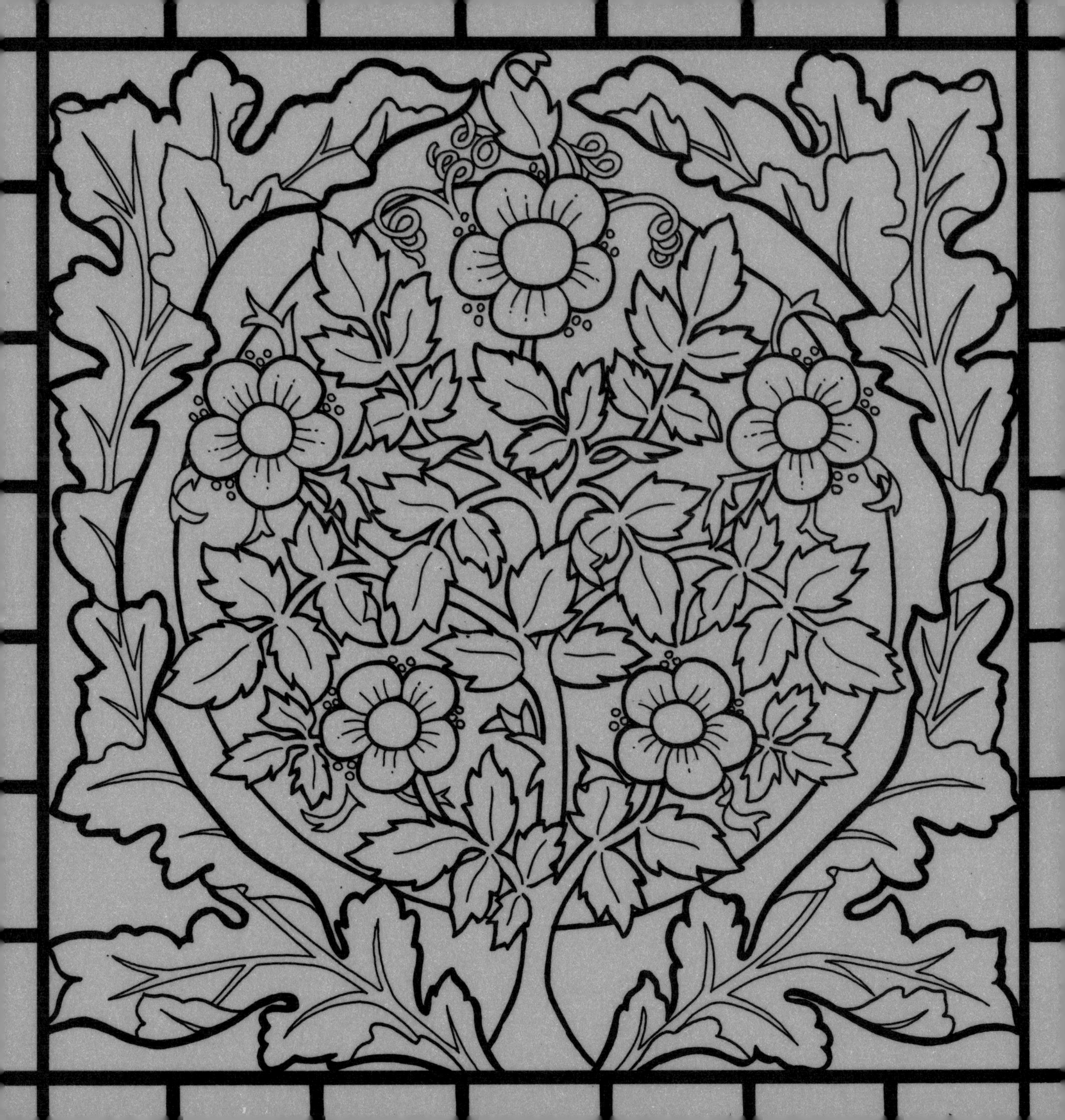

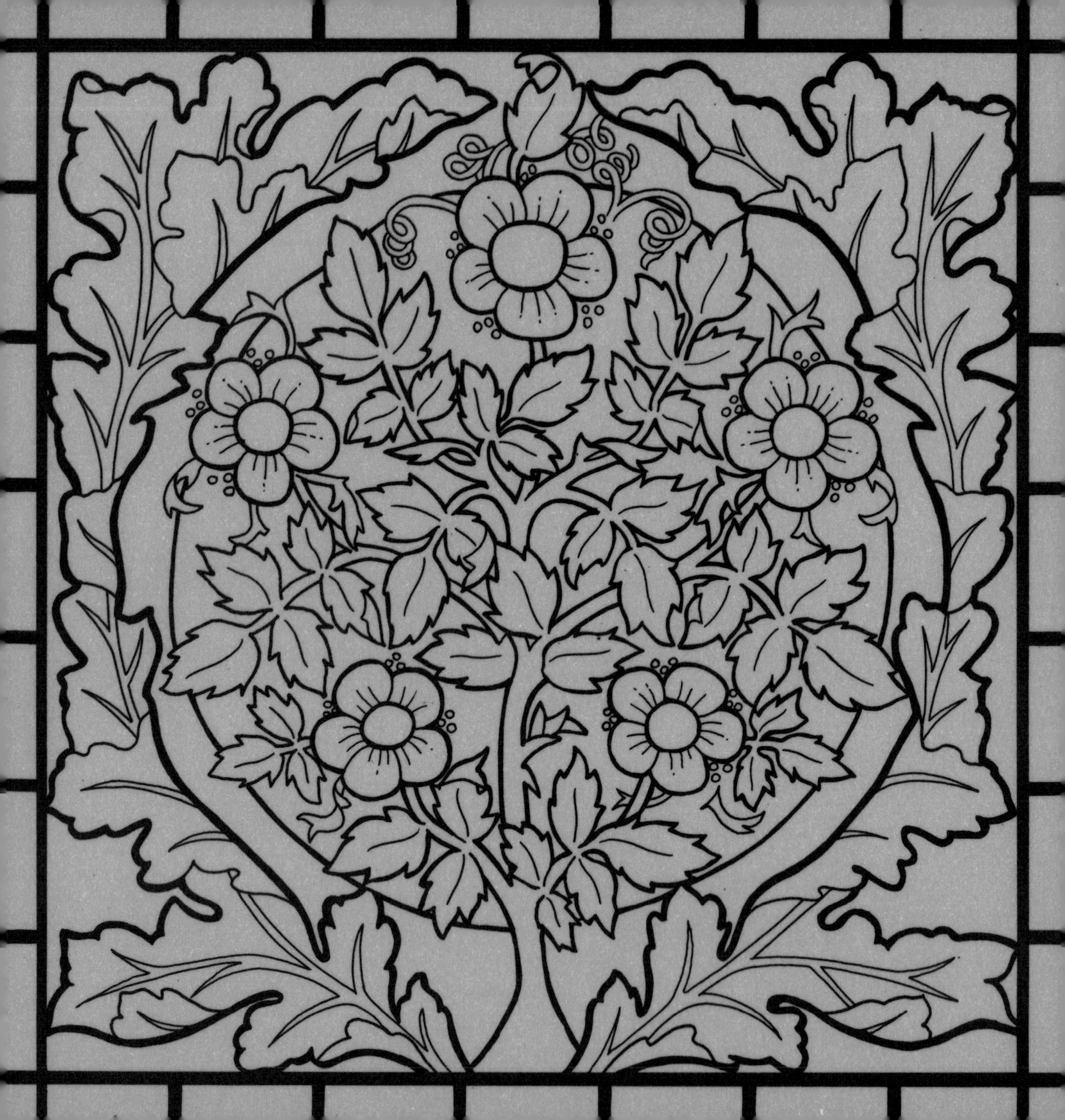

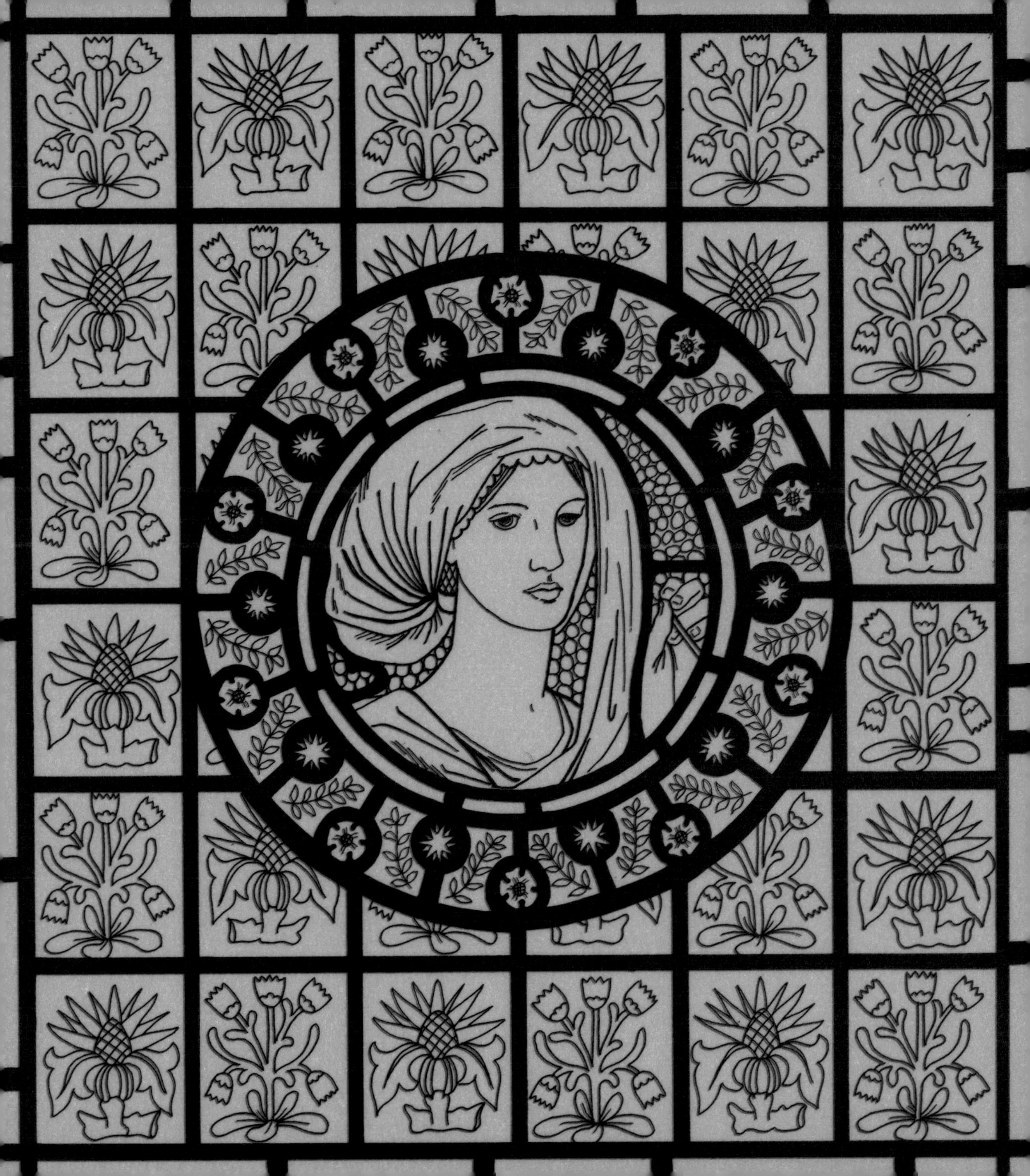

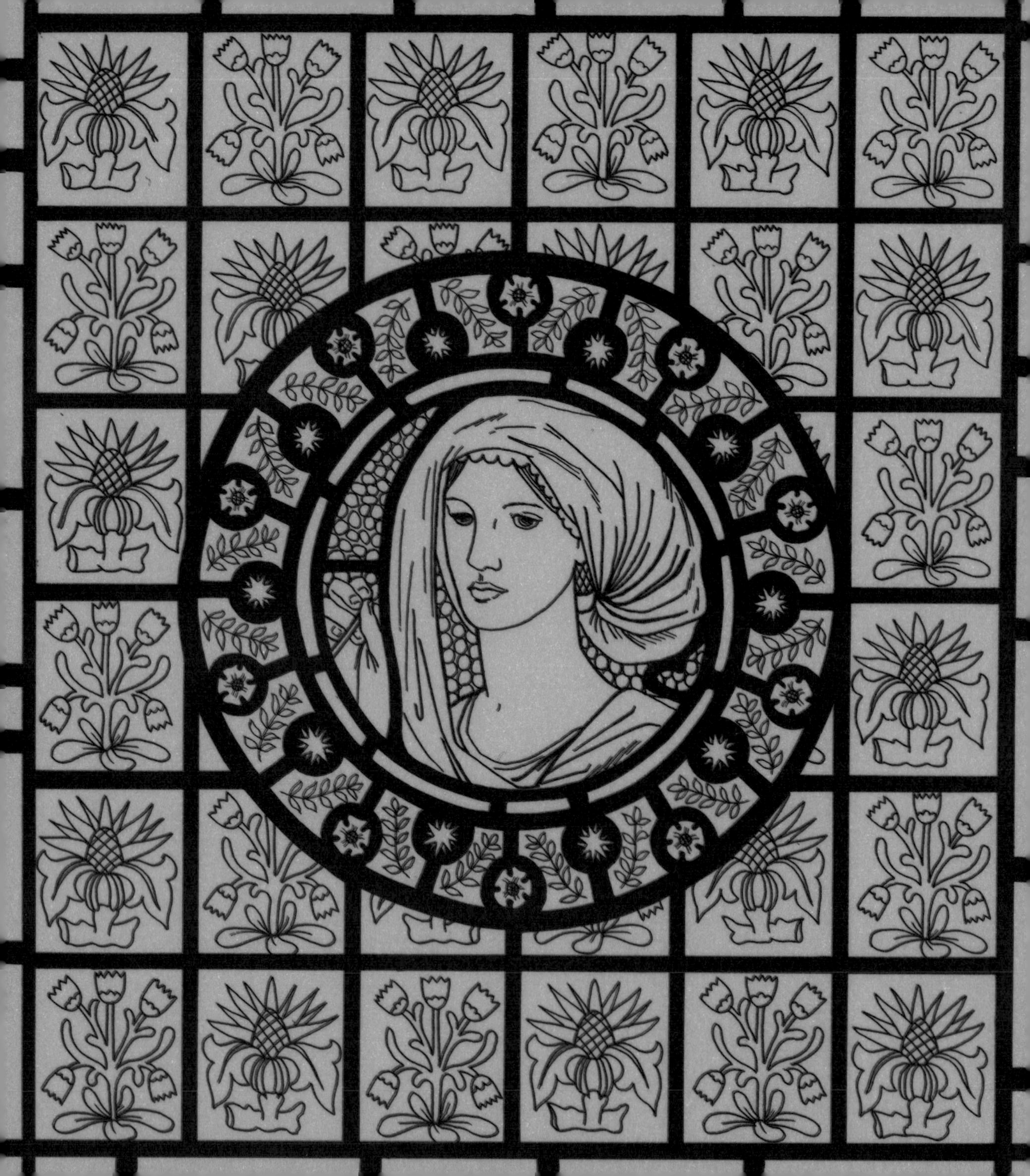

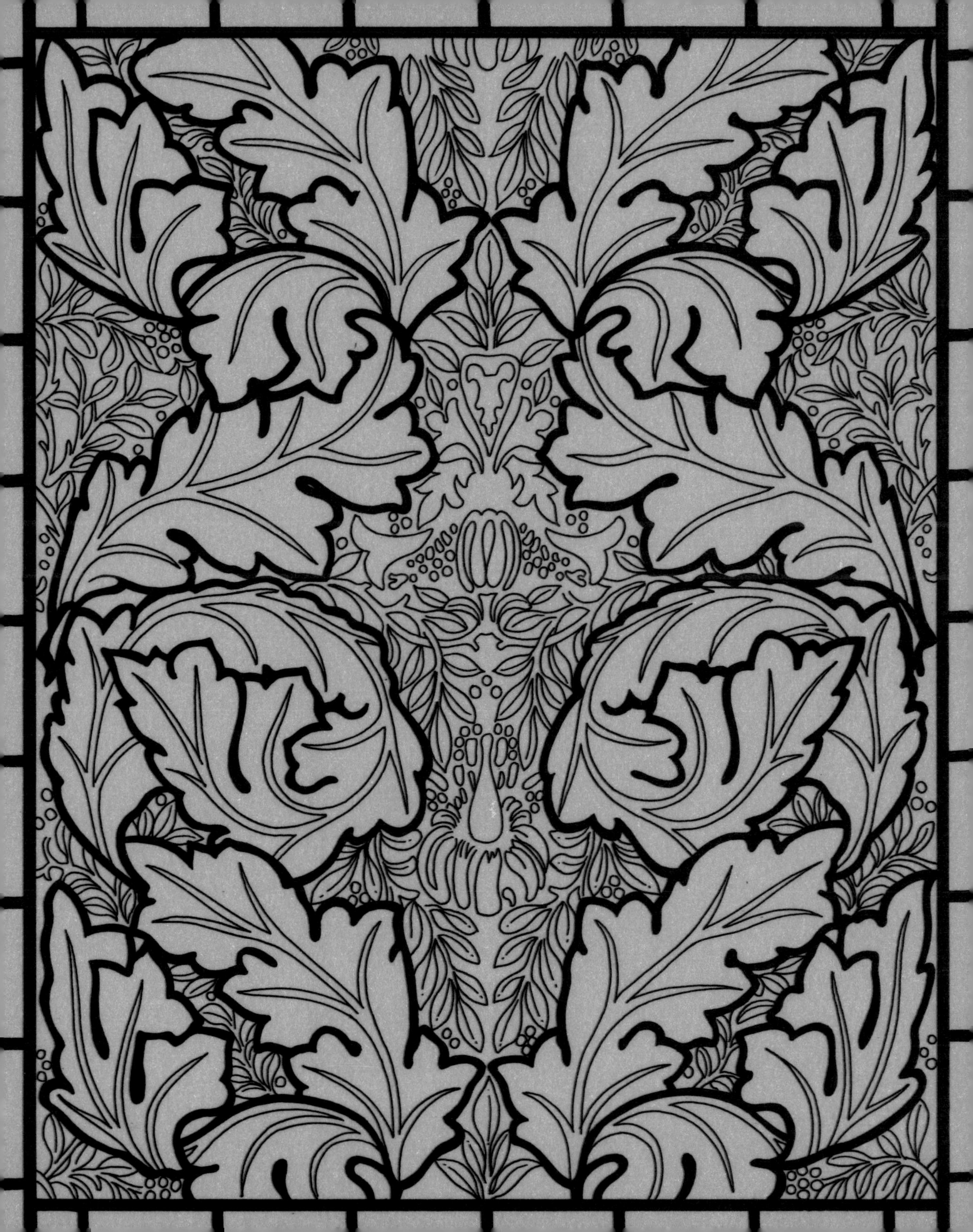

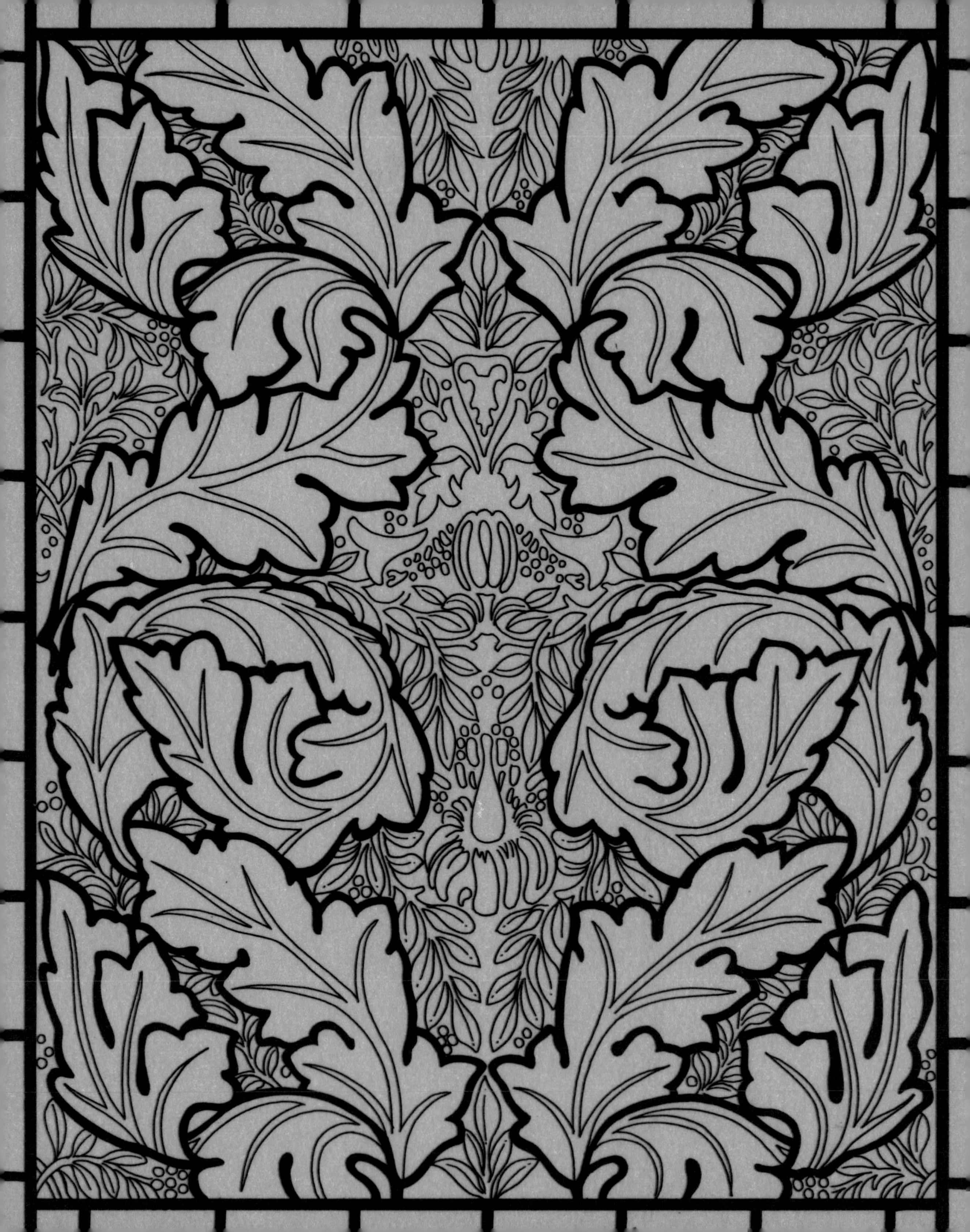

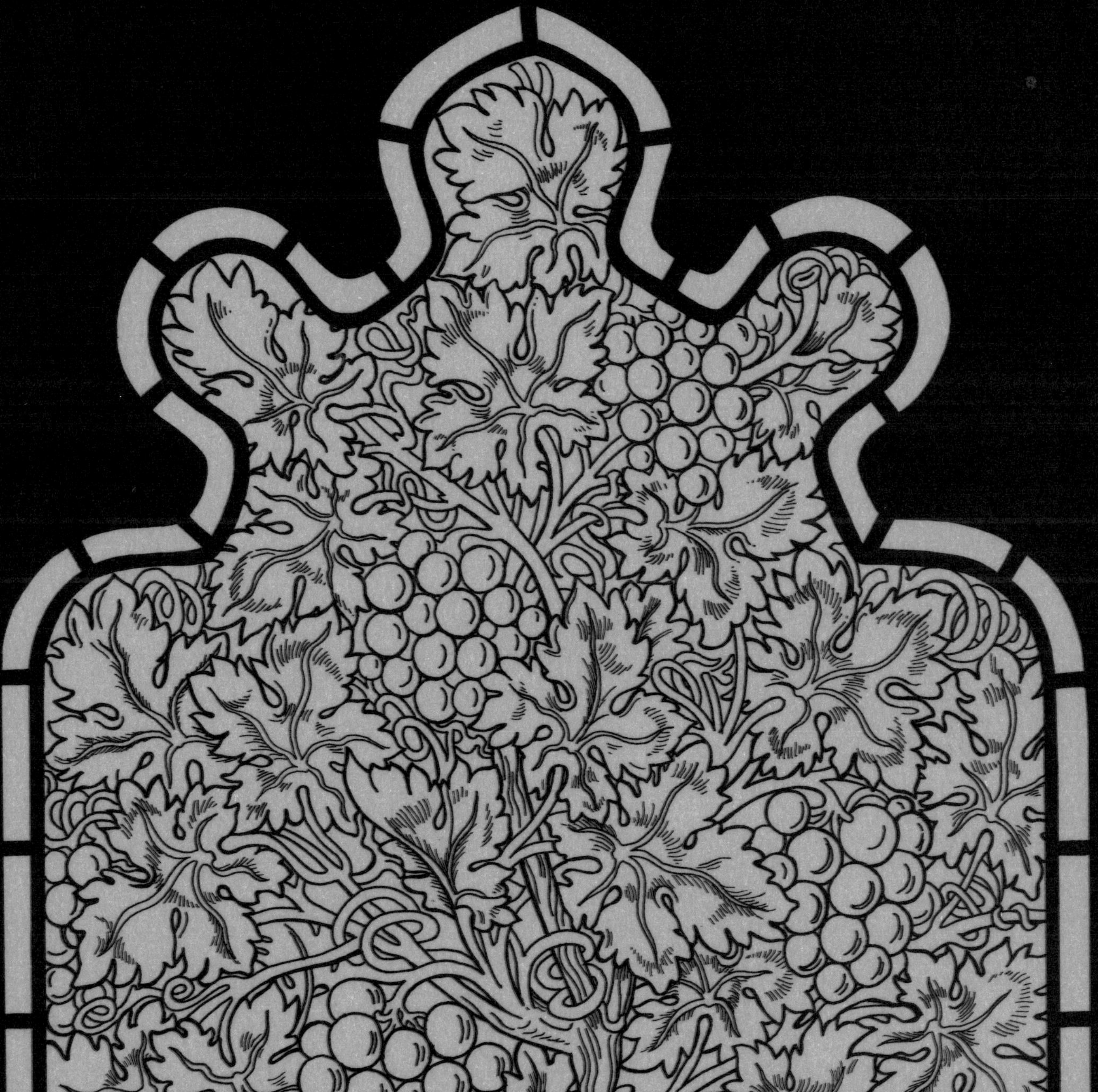

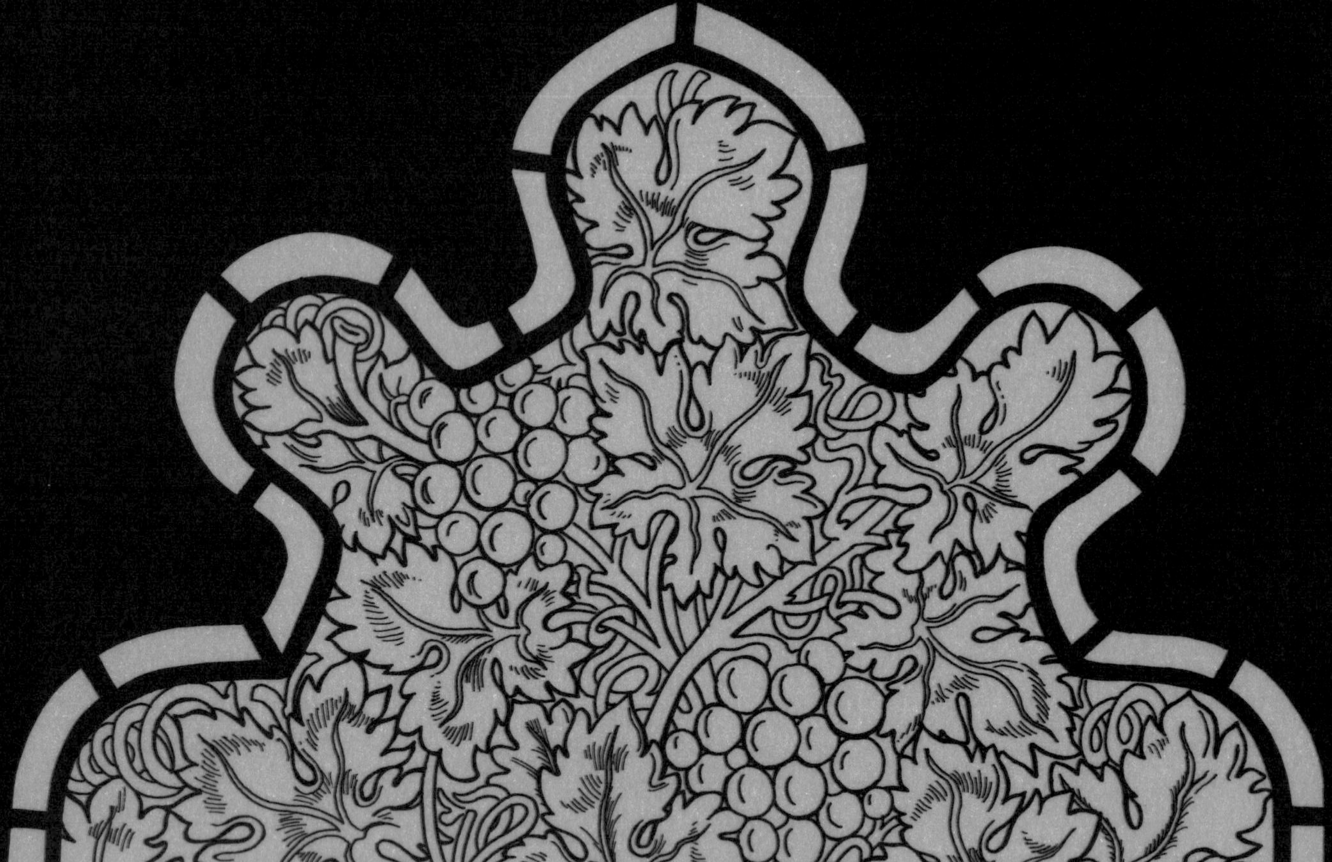

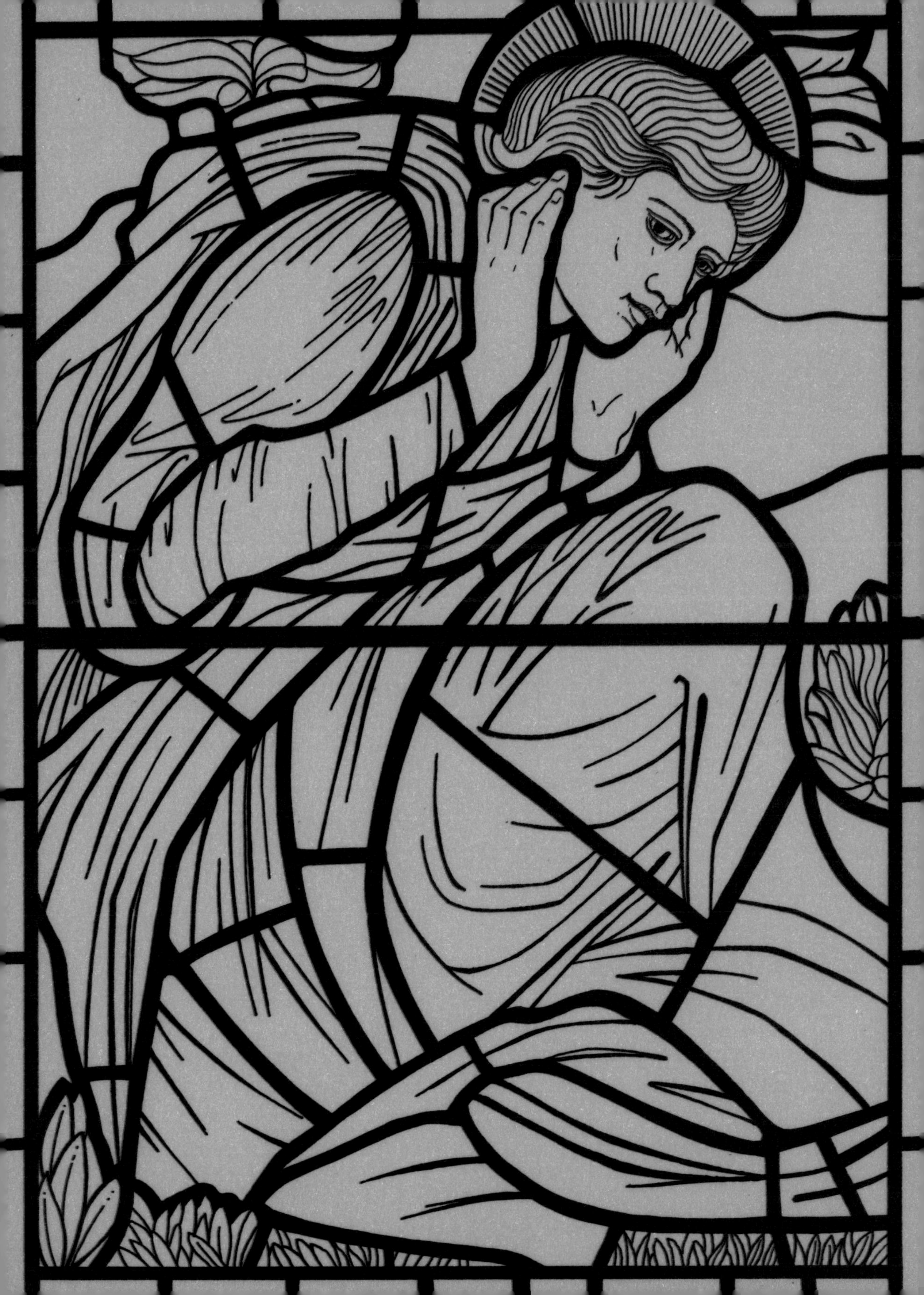

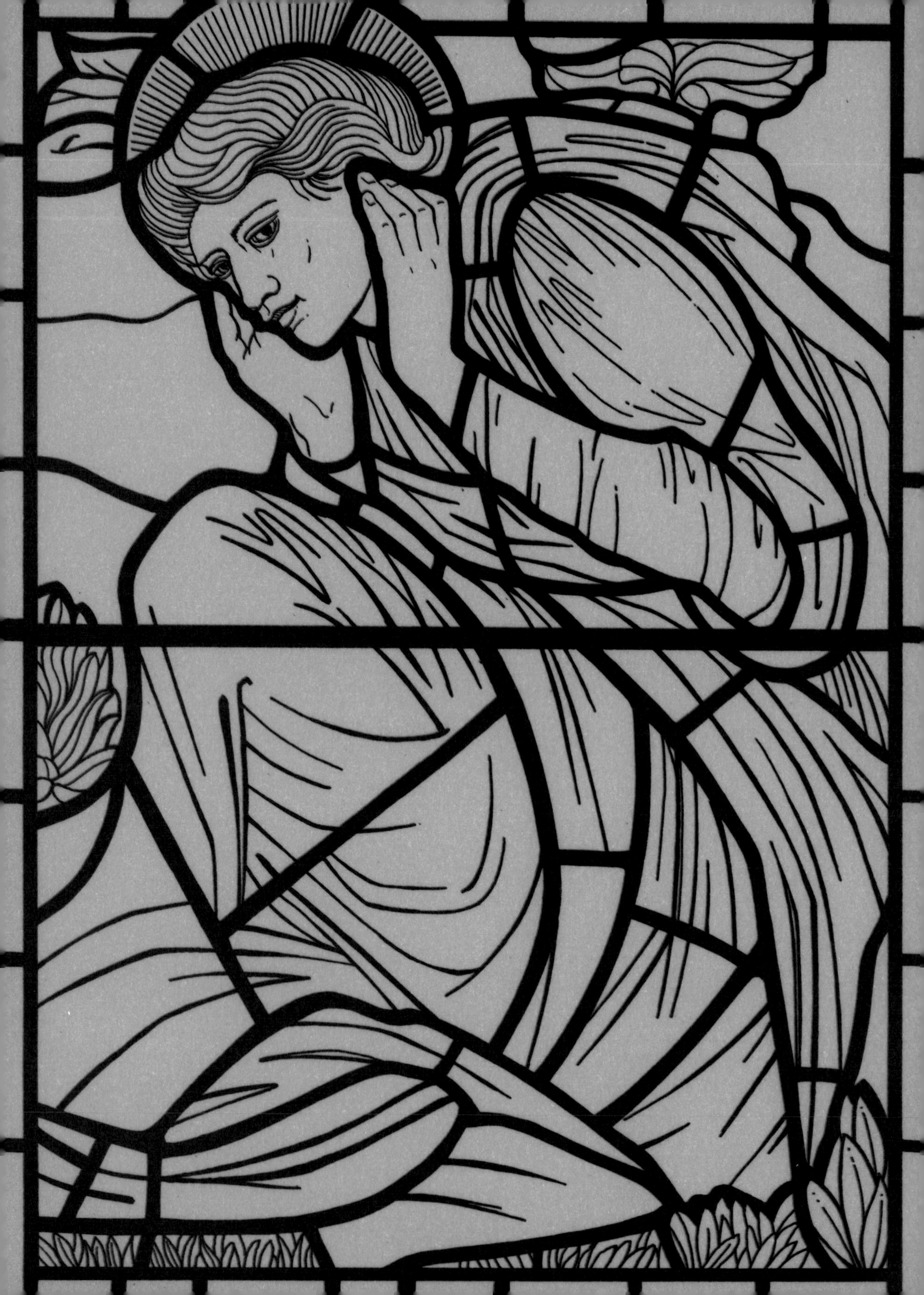

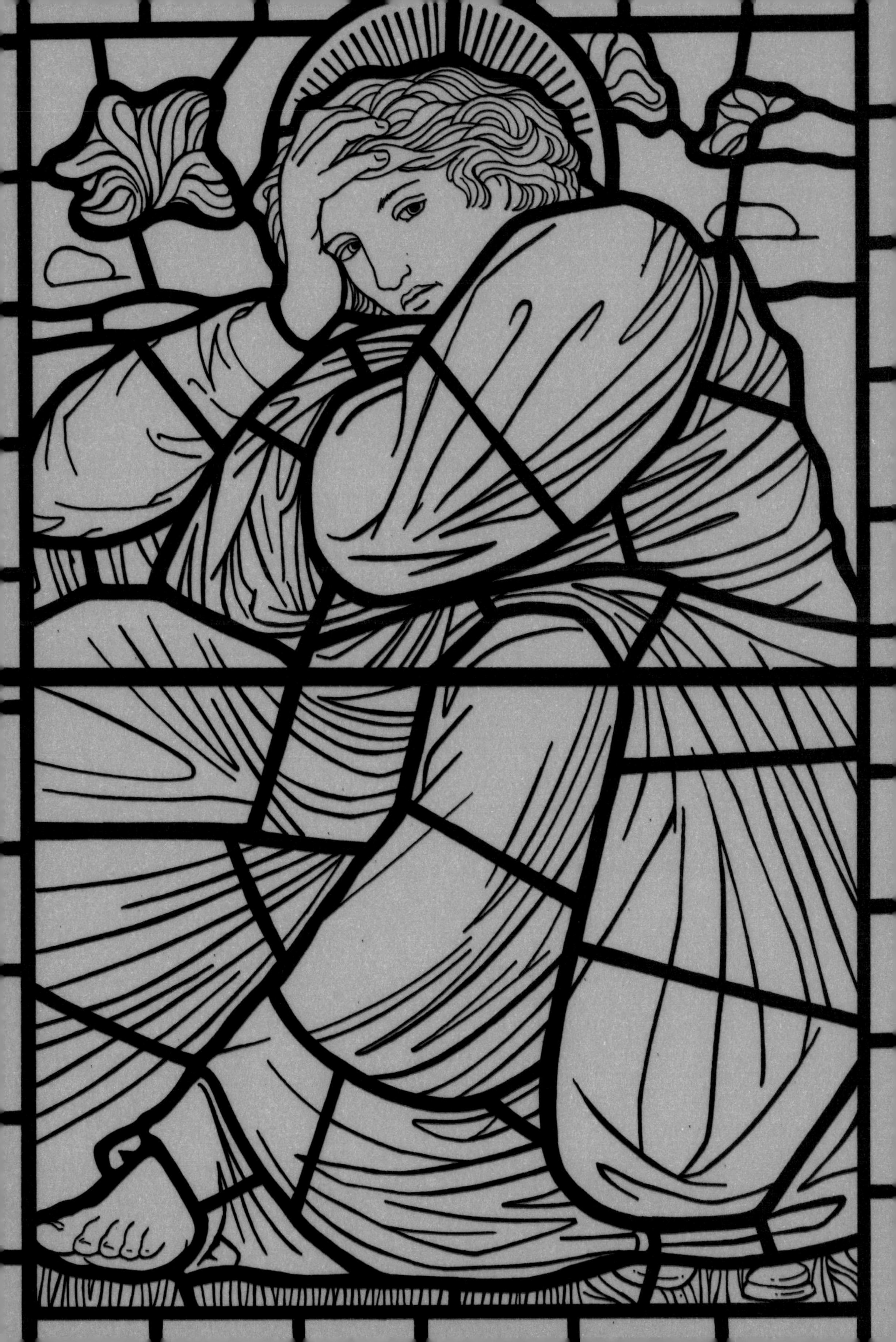

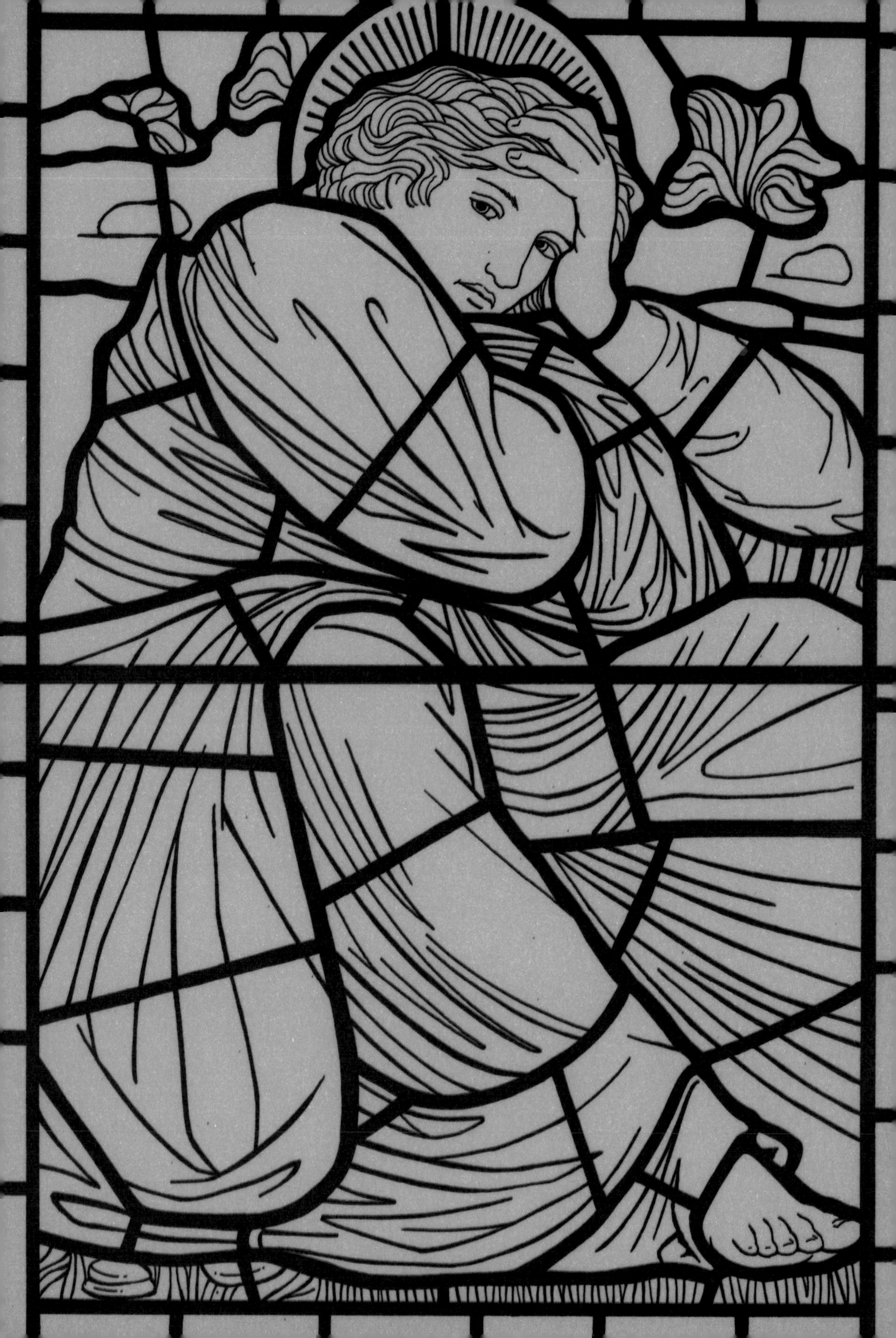

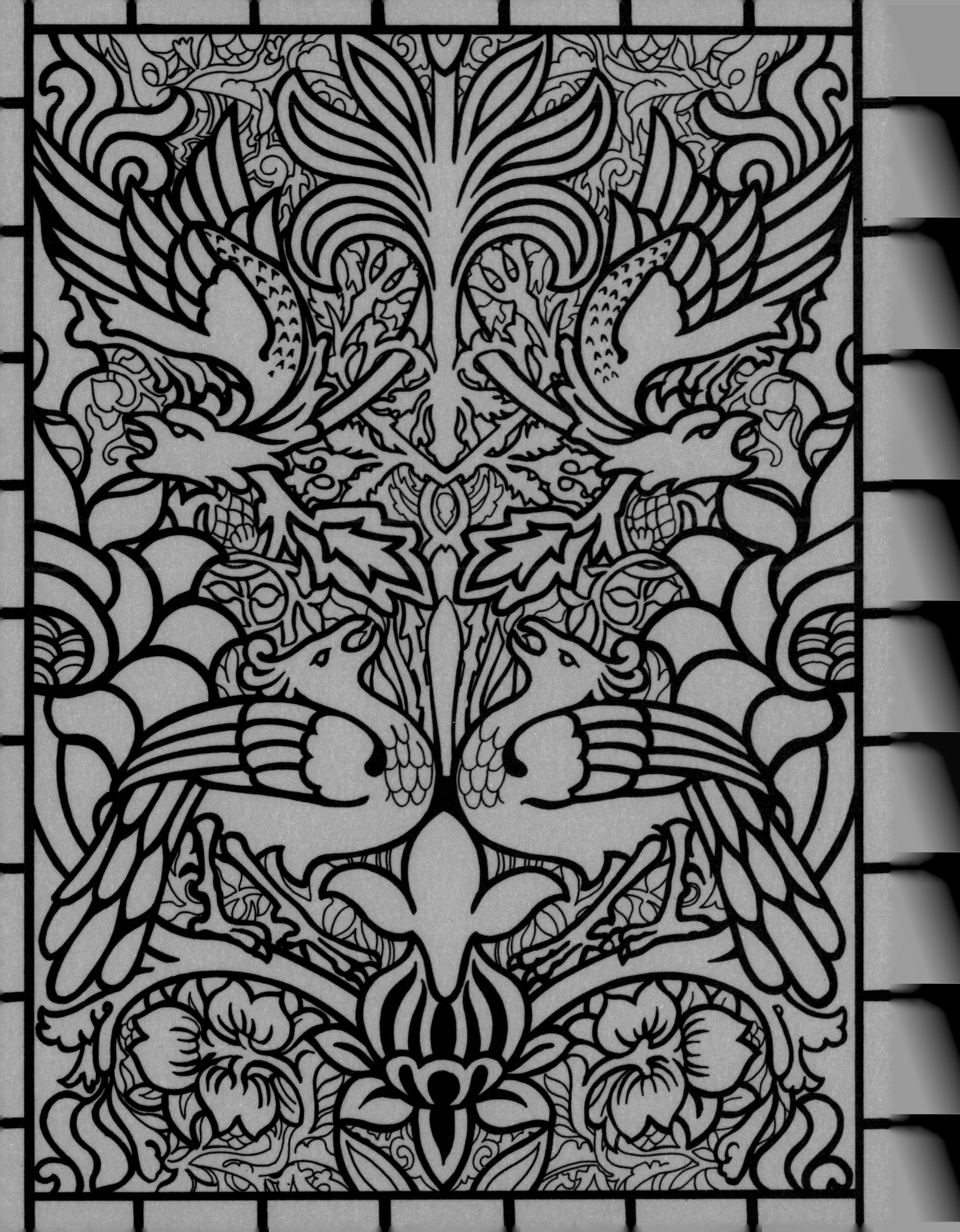

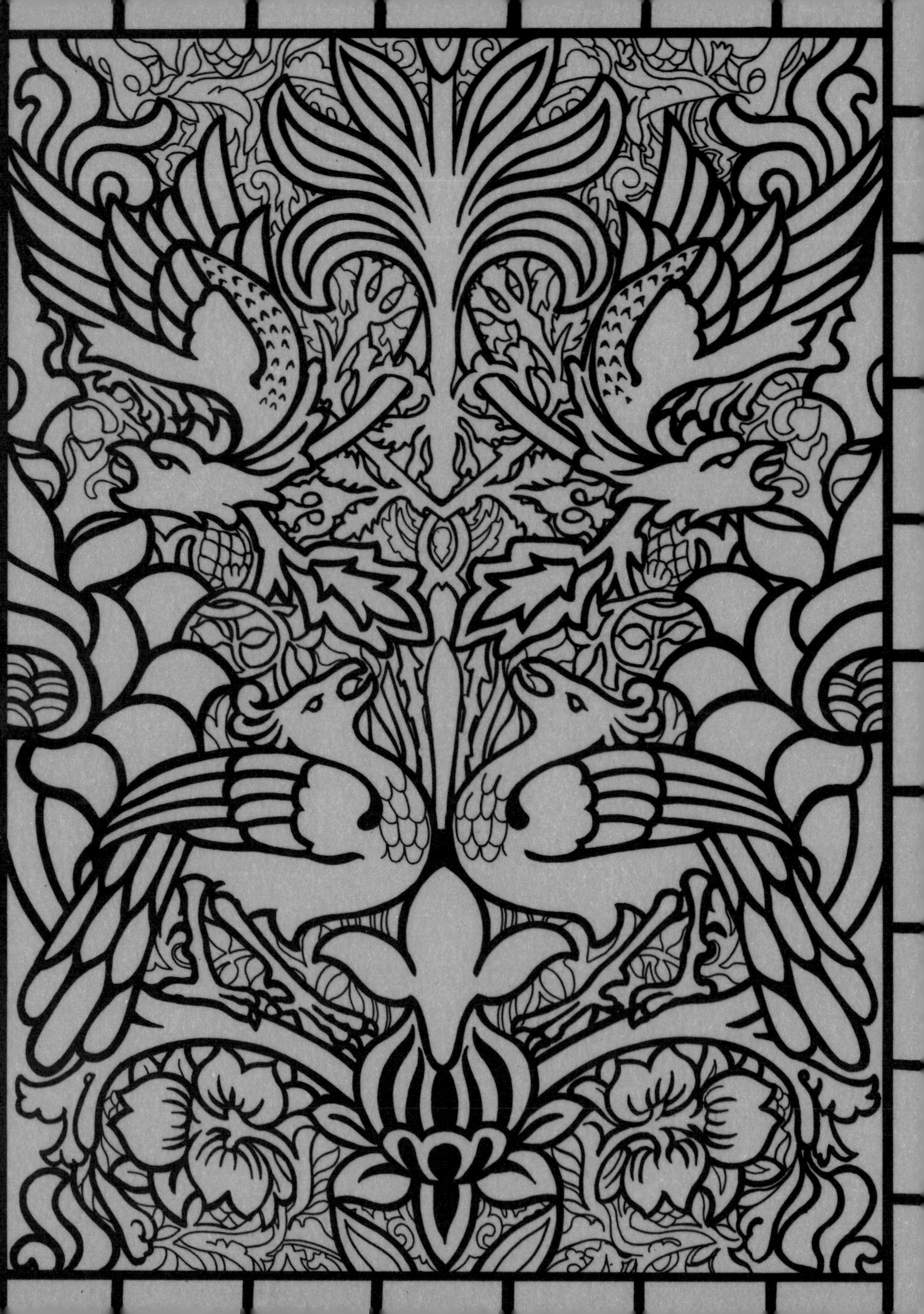